The Church in Iraq

The Catholic University of America Press
Washington, D.C.

The Church in Iraq

Fernando Cardinal Filoni

Translated by Edward Condon

Originally published as *La Chiesa in Iraq: La storia, lo sviluppo, la missione, dagli inizi ai nostri giorni*
© Copyright 2015—Libreria Editrice Vaticana 00120 Città del Vaticano

English translation Copyright © 2017
The Catholic University of America Press

Image on title page spread is a photograph of Mar Mattai monastery in Iraq, and used with permission of Kyselak, on Wikicommons.

Library of Congress Cataloging-in-Publication Data
Names: Filoni, Fernando, author.
Title: The church in Iraq / Fernando Cardinal Filoni ; translated by Edward Condon.
Other titles: Chiesa in Iraq. English
Description: Washington, D.C. : Catholic University of America Press, 2017. | Includes bibliographical references and index.
Identifiers: LCCN 2017007117 | ISBN 9780813229652 (pbk. : alk. paper)
Subjects: LCSH: Catholic Church—Iraq—History. | Iraq—Church history.
Classification: LCC BX1625 .F5513 2017 | DDC 282/.567—dc23
LC record available at https://lccn.loc.gov/2017007117

For the Christians of the Middle East,

The Christians of Iraq,

Martyrs and confessors of the past and present,

And to all persecuted minorities

Contents

Preface

Understanding the history of Christianity in the Middle East, and in particular Mesopotamia—now Iraq—is not a relaxed cultural experience. It requires an approach that understands the reasons behind the dramatic history of that region and appreciates the life, culture, and testimony of faith of its Christians, and also what inspires their deep attachment to their homeland and their implacability toward their enemies.

One must understand the nobility of these people, which has been forged in two fundamental realities: 1) being a minority, which has generated a strong attachment to their own values, origin, and culture; and 2) being the direct heirs of martyrs and confessors of the faith, and consequently bearing the values and the faith of the fathers in a proud and unique way. Those who have lived among them and know their ways cannot but love these people, for understanding makes us capable of sharing and participating in their story. History is itself a victory over ignorance, marginalization, and intolerance; it is a call for respect and to not repeat the mistakes of the past. For this reason, I think that writing this account is helpful.

History tells how these communities have survived centuries of punitive taxation; of inducements and prohibitions; of hate, intolerance, and envy; and, finally, of persecution. All this these Christians have survived, with incredible stamina, a genius for practical and cultural adaption, and an unyielding faith. But when the Lord returns, will he find any faith left in this land?

This volume, therefore, seeks to offer a timely understanding of the birth, evolution, and development of the Christian community in Mesopotamia; and also of its beauty, and the crises and humiliations that explain, in their sociopolitical context, the very strong temper and witness of faith in the face of the current persecution. This Christian community, as a community dating back to the Apostolic era, brings with it the accumulated inheritance of twenty centuries of love for Christ and the Church, and is willing to forsake everything, rather than kneel before the powers of the day.

It is a heroic church, as Popes Benedict XVI and Francis have called it. Without it—and we may say this of all the churches of the Middle East, which have left similar footprints—the region would not be the same. This is without even thinking of the many other ethnic and religious minorities, often persecuted and suffering, in this land. This region is a mosaic of nationalities, religions, and confessions, without which it would have been destroyed forever; this truth is also recognized by eminent Muslim authorities, and even ordinary citizens, who have often repeated it to me. While this is truly positive, yet we must add to this the necessity of facilitating the permanent establishment and daily lives of these minorities.

When, on August 10, 2014, Pope Francis sent me as his personal representative to Iraq to encounter, to talk to, to see, to caress, to pray with, and to stand in solidarity with the victims of the Islamic extremism of ISIS, it was a tremendously emotional experience.

This book was conceived as a testimonial to those victims, to the men and women, Christian and non-Christian, whom I met, and to say thank you to them: thank you for your courage! And thanks also to those who, with sacrifice and love, try to lighten their burdens of fear and anxiety. May they never lessen in their courage, and, together, hope.

This is my most ardent desire in completing this work.

The Church in Iraq

The Geopolitical Context

On June 29, 2014, the first day of Ramadan, Abu Bakr al-Baghdadi proclaimed the birth of the caliphate of the "Islamic State," in eastern Syria, along the border with Iraq. The jihadist insurgence continued with victories and massacres. This campaign was something that residents of Mosul had already been aware of for some time, and they could sense something was changing. The sympathies of Mosul's Sunni population, unhappy with the Shiite dominated politics of Baghdad and nostalgic for the old Baathist regime, were evident. Wahhabist radicals from Saudi Arabia had long been active in the city, even during the reign of Saddam Hussein, and posed an ongoing security concern, often fomenting unrest and attacks against Christians. In July 2004, Islamic terrorists had attacked the bishop of the Chaldeans, Paulos Faraj Rahho, burning down his residence. He was kidnapped and brutally murdered in March of 2008, along with three of his companions, who were ruthlessly killed during his abduction. One year earlier, in June 2007, a Chaldean priest, Ragheed Ganni, and three subdeacons had been murdered; and the Chaldean cathedral and the Dominican church were attacked, as were other buildings belonging to Syrian Catholics and Armenians. Kidnappings and threats against Christian families were innumerable, and during the nights they were sent demands to either convert to Islam or leave Mosul. During the same period, the Syrian Catholic archbishop's house was burned down, as were several Orthodox places of worship.

Mosul, for a truly long time, has been a point of encounter for the rich multiplicity of human cultures, languages, and traditions that have always lived in northern Iraq. Within the territory of Mosul lie the remains, almost unexplored, of the ancient, biblical city of Nineveh. A few kilometers to the southeast one can find the ruins of Nimrud, which was the capital of the Assyrian Empire as early as the eighth century BC, of which the local people still speak quietly as the high point of their civilization. The city is also the last major Sunni outpost before the autonomous region of Iraqi Kurdistan—which opens to the northeast on vast plains bathed by the Great Zab, the river that runs through it as a wide semicircle from the east to the north—and the Turkish border. The Great Zab then flows to the south up to the 36th parallel and the Tigris, drawing a fertile triangle where Christians and non-Christians have lived together for many years. This plain, toward Mosul, is called the Plain of Nineveh, and is considered the breadbasket of Mesopotamia. Its conquest was essential for all the armies that have tried to enter the heart of Mesopotamia and push through to Persia and beyond.

Iraqi territory, which today extends from the eastern borders of Syria to those of western Iran, penetrates between those two countries as a wedge and is divided along it entire length by two major rivers, the Euphrates and the Tigris. It was seat of several great civilizations: from the Sumerians to the Akkadians, the Babylonians, and the Assyrians. Who cannot recall the names of great cities like Ur, Susa, Eridu, Uruk, Larsa, Babylon, Assur, Nineveh, Mari, and Nimrud, whose histories and cultures are the root of civilizations stretching forward to the present day? Mesopotamian Iraq has no natural boundaries, but only those lines left by the end of the First World War and the decomposition of the Ottoman Empire, when the peace negotiations of Paris (1919), and then Sèvres (1920), traced the political geography of the Middle East.[1] Kurdistan, a vast mountainous region situated between Turkey, Iran, Iraq, and Syria, was not recognized as an independent state, but was divided between the surrounding countries. Though granted extensive autonomy by the Treaty of Sèvres, along with a number of safeguards for the protection of Christians and other ethnic and religious minorities,[2] these were sacrificed to the interests of the new states with the Treaty of Lausanne on July 24, 1923.[3] The Council of the League of Nations, on December 16, 1925, formally recognized the frontier between Iraq and Turkey, giving the Hakkari region (Kurdish-Assyrian) to Turkey, and the north of Mosul, up to Amadiya, to Iraq. The Ottoman Kurdistan was thus fragmented, creating a secular irredentism which has known long years of fighting the central powers in Istanbul, Baghdad, Damascus, and Teheran up to the present day. As the dream of an independent Kurdistan vanished, so too did those of even a modest enclave for Assyrian Christians (including Qochanis, Dehoc, and Amadiya); and so Kurds and Christians saw themselves sacrificed to the international interests of the British and French, who were the colonial powers, and to the new states so recently created. This was also the beginning of a wave of migration abroad and among the surrounding new countries. In Iraq the emigration was mainly directed toward Mosul and Baghdad, although the largest Christian community lived on the Plain of Nineveh and in Iraqi Kurdistan, with some large villages populated almost entirely by Syrian Catholics and Orthodox, Chaldeans and Assyrians. Non-Christian minorities

1. See, for example, Agnes de Dreuzy, *The Holy See and the Emergence of the Modern Middle East: Benedict XV's Diplomacy in Greater Syria, 1914–1922* (Washington, D.C.: The Catholic University of America Press, 2016).
2. Treaty of Sèvres, August 10, 1920, art. 62.
3. See M. Galletti, *Le Kurdistan et ses chrétiens* (Paris: Editions du Cerf, 2010), 140.

were gathered in Shaikhan, Lalish, and Sinjar, especially all of the Yazidis, Shabaks, Turkmen, and Mandaeans.

After the creation of a new political structure under the British mandate in 1920,[4] Iraq won substantial and fundamental freedoms in October of 1923, notwithstanding some remaining military and economic constraints imposed by the mandated power. In Iraq, the borders had been dictated more by the logic of interests rather that of peoples and their religious and cultural traditions. Moreover, Britain had supplanted France, and, through the adoption of the so-called Hashemite policy,[5] established a kingdom attentive to the wishes of London and entrusted to Faisal I, while Syria was placed under French mandate. Iraq, in truth, had never been a geopolitical reality, nor inhabited by an identifiable single people, even if there was a tradition of independence. It was, rather, a trophy for its conquerors and a collapsed empire, co-inhabited for centuries by several different nationalities, tribes, religions, and cultures, with an uncertain desert border on one side and Iran on the other.

An emir was installed as a symbol of national identity around which to build and ensure the unity of its people; he was assisted by a parliament and an administration fashioned more in the European style than the Ottoman tradition. This led to a confusion of roles, and to the military autocracy that controlled Iraq for so many years, and which tried to impose some cohesion upon the country, amid riots and uprisings.[6] Sunni Baathists, who were also Hashemites, would never yield authority to any truly democratic process as this would inevitably empower the Shia majority living in the south-central region of Iraq; and the Kurds of the northern region would never accept either Sunni or Shia control. Rather, Sunni Baathist governance was exercised by allow-

4. The Kingdom of Iraq was created on October 1, 1919.
5. See F. Filoni, *La Chiesa nella terra di Abramo* (Milan, Italy: BUR Biblioteca Universale Rizzoli, 2008), 142 ff.
6. Ibid., 143.

ing some administrative autonomy for the Shiites, but without opposition to Bagdad. In the wake of the Anglo-American, later the Allied, invasion of 2003, which deposed the regime of Saddam Hussein, the Shiites assumed the leadership of the country and began to exert a heavy influence on government, unacceptable to the Sunnis who have reacted with more than a decade of bloody violence. The old Shia-Sunni theological dispute, along with cultural and tribal rivalries, places the two communities in a constant and unresolvable conflict, always ready to explode if the opportunity arises.

The smoldering tensions between the two communities, first the Shia, with their most holy places in Najaf and Karbala, and second the Sunni, in the central-western region (including Baghdad and Mosul), are politically fueled from outside by Shiite Iran and the other Sunni Arab countries, who, in this way, keep the divide open and cause a constantly fragile and uncertain future. In the north, Kurdish separatism is the third largest political block in Iraq, with the Kurds situated between Sunni territory toward the Turkish border on one side and Shiite Iran on the other.[7] In the context of these three dominant political and religious forces, small minorities have no real role and are forced to defend their rights, their *ius soli*, their history, their cultures and traditions, all while trying to stay peacefully apart from the conflicts of the larger communities.

7. Today, the centers of economic development are, in the north, Dehoc and Arbil, under the historic sway of the Barzani family; to the east, Sulaymaniyah, which is under the influence of the Talabani family.

Chapter 1

The Ancient Christian Community

1. Initial Evangelization and Formation of the Church of the East

Tradition has it that Christianity first arrived in the region during the first and second centuries AD through the preaching of St. Thomas the Apostle, and then his disciples Addai and Mari. This tradition is commonly held from Upper Mesopotamia (Osroene,[1] Nineveh, Hatra, and Adiabene[2]) through Lower Mesopotamia (Seleucia-Ctesiphon, Babylon, and Basra), and the territory of the Parthian Empire of the Arsacids (247 BC–224 AD), which was east of the Euphrates and extended from the Tigris into Media and Persia. As early as the Acts of the Apostles, we read that among those who heard the preaching at Pentecost in their own language were "residents of Mesopotamia" (Acts 2:9). This cultural memory, or tradition, of Thomas the Apostle and his disciples bringing the Gospel to the region, and from there moving into southern Mesopotamia, had already taken root by the third century and was reported by Eusebius of Caesarea[3]

1. The kingdom of Osroene was centered on its capital Edessa, today Urfa in modern Turkey.
2. This covered the region between the Great Zab and Little Zab rivers, and was governed from Arbil in what is modern Iraqi Kurdistan.
3. Eusebius of Caesarea in Palestine was a bishop and writer. He is regarded as a father of the Church; he also served as an adviser to and biographer of the Emperor Constantine.

(265–340 AD) in his *Ecclesiastical History*.[4] The roads to Mesopotamia, starting at the Syrian coast and Damascus, pass through Aleppo on their way to Edessa and Nisibis. Here they could be taken north, into the heart of Anatolia, eastward into the Parthian Empire, or south to Nineveh, Abril, Seleucia-Ctesiphon, and finally to Babylon. The alternative route follows the Euphrates, running through Dura-Europos and along the present Iraqi-Syrian border—which was then where the Roman and Parthian empires met—and enters Mesopotamia from the west, following a southeastern course. The remains of an early Christian house-church in Dura-Europos, found along with fragments of scrolls containing eucharistic prayers, suggest Christian communities were already living there by the second and third centuries. These roads were crisscrossed by armies, traders' caravans, and evangelizers. Sadly, they were also well used, even then, by those fleeing war and devastation, even entire displaced populations. Seleucia-Ctesiphon,[5] the twin cities on the Tigris that were first the Arsacid and then the Sasanian capitals (225–651), lay just southeast of Baghdad and became a center of evangelization for the disciples of Mari, and were, from the second century until 780, first a diocese, then an archdiocese, and finally a patriarchal see[6] for the Church of the East.[7] As was the case in the Roman Empire in the west, the numerous Jew-

4. In Book III, which treats of the apostolic centers of preaching, Eusebius writes that the region was given to Thomas as his field of work. See also J. Habbi, "La Chiesa d'Oriente in Mesopotamia," *Mesopotamia* 27: 211.

5. Seleucia was founded on the right bank of the Tigris by Seleucus I Nicator (312 BC), and Ctesiphon on the left bank of the great river in the second century BC, becoming a bipolar urban complex. This city was the capital of the Parthians and was conquered and destroyed by the Romans in several stages, by the Emperors Trajan (116 AD), Lucius Verus (165 AD), Septimius Severus (198 AD), and Carus (283 AD). In future points throughout the text, "AD" will not be used; all dates are AD unless specifically noted as "BC."

6. See J. Yacoub, *I Cristiani d'Iraq* (Milan: Jaca Book, 2006), 138.

7. The Church of the East is considered a branch of the Syriac Church because of its liturgical use of that language.

ish communities, who had spread across Mesopotamia over the course of centuries, were the first to receive the Good News; and they took it with them along their usual routes of travel, creating a network of expansion for Christianity into the region. This Church, descending from the Apostles, gradually spread out from its original core eastward to Persia, as it did in the north toward the Caucasus; and in the first three centuries the primitive episcopal sees enjoyed a very great degree of autonomy. The first of these sees was under bar Aggai (237–336) who, as bishop of Seleucia-Ctesiphon, established a *catholicate*[8] with his see as the head of the local ecclesiastical community. At that time, the Eastern Church existed on the very eastern fringes of the Roman Empire, beyond the borders of the Roman province of Syria; and scholars believe that, in terms of ecclesiastical hierarchy, it was formally subject neither to Rome nor to Constantinople. Indeed, from the beginning, the Apostolic and post-Apostolic Churches of the region have always maintained a certain separation as a natural result of geographical and political circumstances. This is not to say that they lacked contact with other Churches, with whom they had exchanges on spiritual and liturgical matters, and with the Jewish-Christian communities, with whom they discussed issues of ecclesiastical organization and theology, fostering discussion and agreement among them. While not hierarchically linked, the Christian communities of Mesopotamia may well have been in contact with the other neighboring Churches, including the great Apostolic sees of Antioch, Alexandria, Jerusalem, Constantinople, and Rome. Until the end of the third century, the unity which existed among the different Churches was guaranteed not by ecclesiastical structure but by the unity of the faith, based on an adherence to the Apostolic tradition and

8. A *catholicate* is a particular structure in the Churches of the East, meaning the territory of a *catholicos*. While there is no direct equivalent in the Latin Church, it can loosely be seen as being a more autonomous variety of an archdiocesan province.

the celebration of the Eucharist, which together formed the great theological and sacramental bonds. And it was through these two, Apostolic tradition and the liturgy of the Eucharist, that the Church of the East expanded into the more far-flung Roman provinces and neighboring kingdoms beyond the Euphrates.

The expansion of Christianity into eastern Syria and Osroene, conquered by the Emperor Trajan in around 116, can be documented in the first half of the second century. The evangelization of that kingdom is most commonly attributed to Addai, while Mari went south to preach to the Parthians in their capital, Seleucia-Ctesiphon.[9] Addai's work of evangelization is believed to have been carried on by his disciple Aggai, who was later martyred. From a purely historical point of view, we can establish the presence of Christian communities in Nisibis (between Edessa and Mosul) from the testimony of Abercius, bishop of Hierapolis, who was martyred under Marcus Aurelius in 167.[10] Historical documents regarding the period of initial evangelization and the formation of the first Christian communities are somewhat more scarce, but the unbroken tradition of the region gives credibility to the so-called *Anaphora of Addai and Mari* which categorically asserts the existence of well-structured and liturgically organized communities. The *Anaphora of Addai and Mari*, which is written in Syro-Aramaic, is one of the oldest known Eucharistic liturgical texts, dating back to the primitive Church, and was clearly composed with the intention of celebrating the Eucharist in full continuity with the Last Supper, and according to the intention of Christ and the tradition of the Church.[11]

9. According to the Church of the East, Addai and Mari were two of the seventy-two disciples of Christ, and later missionaries and founders of Churches.

10. See I. Ortiz de Urbina, "Le origini del cristianesimo in Edessa," *Gregorianum* 15 (1934): 83–4.

11. It is still in use today in the Assyrian Church of the East. Its likely date of codification is placed at around the year 200. The distinguishing feature of this Anaphora is that the prayers of consecration are not present as a narrative

This particular Anaphora,[12] which was used by the communities of Edessa, as well as those as far south as Seleucia-Ctesiphon, indicates—through its attribution to Addai and Mari—the way in which the two were held to be not only evangelizers and disciples, but figures of authority as well. Eusebius of Caesarea, in his *Ecclesiastical History*, speaks of Edessa hosting the Synod of Osroene in 197, which met to discuss the date of Easter.[13] From the synod's text it is clear that the various Christian communities were governed by leaders who exercised the same functions as bishops. This evidence suggests that the churches of the Mesopotamian region were an important grouping around a site of particular importance, and indicates a transition from a primitive stage to a more structured phase in life of the community, typical of the third century. In addition to Eusebius (writing in 325), there are also the accounts of the Christian community in Edessa centering on the *Mandylion*,[14] a cloth on which Christ's face was supernaturally imprinted, which was famous enough to attract the curiosity of Egeria,[15] who was a pilgrim there in 384.

---

but "in a dispersed euchological way, that is, integrated in successive prayers of thanksgiving, praise and intercession." (Pontifical Council for the Promotion of Christian Unity, *Guidelines for Admission to the Eucharist Between the Chaldean Church and the Assyrian Church of the East* (July 20, 2001).

12. It remains one of the three traditional Anaphoras in use in the Assyrian Church of the East.

13. According to Eusebius, the first regional synod to exercise vigilance over doctrine and practice in their communities was celebrated around the year 172, just to "examine … new doctrines and to find them profane, they condemned the heretical content and expelled, by excommunication from the Church, those who followed them" (*Ecclesiastical History*, V, 16, 10). He also confirms that, around the year 190, synods and other assemblies of local bishops were held on the question of Easter, with their conclusions sent to Pope Victor (ibid., V, 23, 2–4; 24ff.), bishop of Rome from 189 to 199. It was during his pontificate that the controversy on the celebration of Easter arose; Pope Victor wrote to the bishops' conferences and received numerous responses, including one from the bishops of the kingdom of Osroene.

14. This cloth, believed to be a miraculous depiction of the face of Christ, was presented to King Abgar of Edessa.

15. Egeria (also known as Etheria) wrote an account of her long pilgrim-

We must also consider the binding force of, and the unity suggested by, the common liturgical language of the region, Syriac, which is part of the Aramaic group, and which was used among the general population. It is a dialect of Phoenician and Hebrew, widely used by the Assyrians and in Edessa, where it became the literary language of the Church; it remained the common language at least until the eighth century, when Arabic was imposed by the new conquerors. Today it is still a living language, as a dialect, among the Assyrian-Chaldean Christian communities of Syria, Iraq, Turkey, and Iran.

2. Heresies, the Separation and Isolation of the Church of the East

There was never a shortage of heresies in Edessa.[16] It was here that Bardesanes was born to wealthy Parthian parents, and was educated alongside Abgar IX (179–216), the heir to the throne of Osroene.[17] He converted to Christianity by listening to the homilies of Hystaspes, the bishop of Edessa and helped Abgar establish the first Christian kingdom. While he produced many works of his own against the gnostics of his time, his own theories were infected by Babylonian astrology and refuted by Ephrem the Syrian.[18] He probably died around 222 in Edessa, having witnesses the defeat of the Osroene kingdom and its ab-

age to the Holy Land, where she stayed three years; she gives interesting descriptions of her travels through Bithynia, Edessa, Judea, Sinai, and Egypt. See Etheria, *The Pilgrimage of Etheria*, trans. M. L. McClure and C. L. Feltoe (London: Society for Promoting Christian Knowledge, 1919).

16. Heretical sects, including the Marcionites and the Valentinians, spread through the area between the second and third centuries, while the *Diatessaron* of the gnostic Tatian (composed in about 180) was widely circulated by the fifth century.

17. Sextus Julius Africanus refers to him as "the Parthian," Porphyrius as "the Babylonian," while Hippolytus of Rome called him "the Armenian," and Ephrem the Syrian "the Aramean."

18. In addition to many poems and hymns composed in Syriac, Barde-

sorption into the Roman Empire in 216. Further south at about that same time, Mani was born to a prominent Iranian family[19] and would join the Mandaeans.[20] Educated according to their principles, he came to know Christianity through the Gospels as well as through many different apocryphal New Testament accounts, which he harmonized with Zoroastrian doctrine. Believing himself to be the divinely inspired prophet and leader of a new religion, he set off to preach in the East, going as far as Balochistan, now spread across parts of modern Pakistan, Iran, and Afghanistan. This trip was possible because of the ascent of the Sassanian dynasty to power in the Persian Empire, replacing the Arsacids in 225. In 242, in Ctesiphon, King Shapur I granted Mani permission to organize his new religion and to preach his doctrine across all of Mesopotamia.[21] It quickly spread to Basra, Babylon, and the kingdom of Adiabene up to Nisibis, while his followers spread as far as Syria, Egypt, and the Caucasus. Denounced by the Zoroastrians, and having lost favor with the Sassanid king Bahram I, Mani died in prison around the year 277. After his death, his followers were harshly persecuted and scattered to the west and to the east of the Sassanid kingdom, taking their new religion to Africa (where Diocletian promulgated a severe edict against the Manichaeans in 297), Spain, Gaul, and

---

sanes also wrote a *Dialogue against Fate*, which was declared heretical in the fifth century.

19. Mani's birth is recorded as having been on April 14, 216, probably in or near Seleucia-Ctesiphon, which was then the Parthian imperial capital.

20. The Mandaeans, sometimes called the Sabeans, were a gnostic group tracing their origins back to the disciples of John the Baptist. Their interpretation of biblical figures and sources, including the story of Adam, and the ministry of John and the practice of Baptism, produce a separation between the earthly and the heavenly Jesus and a dualistic concept of the world.

21. Mani preached a syncretism among Christianity, Gnosticism, and elements of other religions, including Buddhism. The structure he gave to his Church included a supreme leader based in Babylon, with a hierarchy of twelve apostles, seventy-two masters of truth, and 360 priests and deacons (both men and women).

even to Rome itself. Such was their influence that the synods of the fourth century were largely concerned with the Manichaean heresies. While various emperors passed increasingly punitive legislation, the Church expended an enormous amount of intellectual energy in the long fight against them, including that of Augustine, Leo the Great, Cyril of Jerusalem, and Aphrahat.

If having to combat heresies across the region had the negative effects of sowing division within the Church and of disrupting the evangelization, it also had the positive consequences of inspiring more vivid theological formulations, a huge increase in apologetic writings, and new schools of ascetic thought and practice, all of which undoubtedly enriched the life of the Church. Aphrahat (270–345) was one such example in Mesopotamia and presents a very interesting example in the history of the Church in the third and fourth centuries. He was a figure who contributed to the ecclesiological and literary life of his time, particularly in the ascetic monasticism of Syria and Upper Mesopotamia, of which he was a leading exponent, and which was different from the monasticism of the Egyptian desert. In fact, the communities that arose in the Syrian-Mesopotamian region at that time were an expression of Christianity whose theological formation was very much its own and not yet in regular contact with other cultural currents. These were Churches in which asceticism, in both hermetical and communal forms (of the desert, of the caves, the stylites, the recluses), had a vital role in the development of theological and spiritual thought.[22] Aphrahat, known as "the Sage," a native of Nineveh, embodied several aspects of ecclesial life in the region, first as a monk, then an abbot, and finally a bishop. He is well-known for his collection of twenty-three speeches, known as the *Expositions* or *Demonstrations*, which discuss various aspects of the Christian life: faith, love, humility, prayer, fast-

22. See Benedict XVI, general audience, November 21, 2007. Magisterial documents may be found at http://www.vatican.va/.

ing, the ascetic life, and the relationship between Judaism and Christianity, and which drew upon both the Old Testament and the New Testament.

Aphrahat was also a contemporary of Ephrem the Syrian. Ephrem was born into a Christian family in Nisibis in about 306 and became a hugely significant figure as a theologian, poet, and deacon of his local Church, in which he was vitally active, co-founding a theological school at Nisibis with his bishop, James (303–38), in the year 325, which came to be called the "the Persian School."[23] When the Emperor Jovian surrendered Nisibis to the Persians in 363, Ephrem moved to Edessa, which was still under Roman control, taking with him many of the local Christian community, as well as the school. He remained and preached in Edessa until his death, ten years later. He is especially remembered for his Holy Thursday discourse on the primacy of Peter and for his *Hymn to St. Peter,* in which he wrote: "The Son of God has placed you as the foundation of the Church, so that you will support the weight of all creatures, as He maintains the whole world… (the Church) confesses with you that He is the Son of God."[24] Ephrem's ecclesiology, and deference to the see of that city, was heavily informed by the historical significance of Peter's confession and martyrdom having taken place in Rome.

Ecclesiastical structures in the Mesopotamian region at that time were not unlike those of Syria and Asia Minor, in particular as regards the role of the bishop, who was elected by the consensus of the faithful for the wisdom and the esteem in which they held him, and later was confirmed and consecrated by the bishops of the province; as well as the role of priests, to whom were entrusted the pastoral care of the faithful; and that of dea-

23. The Persian School taught three subjects: philosophy, theology, and medicine.
24. G. Bosio, *Iniziazione ai Padri,* vol. 2 (Turin: Società Editrice Internazionale, 1964), 185.

cons, who functioned as aides to the bishop and who performed works of charity for and on behalf of the community. The ecclesiastical provinces of the time were formed by the missionary process, by language, and by nationality. Within the provinces, synods formed the link between the different bishops and allowed them a measure of pastoral and canonical collaboration. In the third century, across Mesopotamia, as well as Persia, a number of displaced Syrian Christian communities, complete with their own bishops, began to arrive and organize themselves into distinct groups of faith and cult—the communities had been forced to flee as a result of the Sassanian military campaigns. In 325, the Synod of Seleucia met to discuss the issue of episcopal jurisdiction, but it was Catholicos Ishaq who settled the ecclesiastical organization of the province when he convened a further synod in the same city, in about 410, and reordered the dioceses into a great metropolitan, with himself as the Primate of the Church of the East. It was at this later synod that the Church of the East broke hierarchical links to Antioch and the other western bishops, and adopted the canons of the Councils of Nicaea and Constantinople and reaffirmed the See of Seleucia-Ctesiphon as primatial.

The Edict of Constantine in 313 greatly changed the situation for Christians in the Roman Empire, securing them civil rights and religious freedoms, and addressing some of the injustices of the great persecutions.[25] The edict also carried into the provinces of the Eastern Roman Empire (later known as the Byzantine Empire), where the new toleration of Christianity was also to be observed; this had a great impact on the social and religious life of the Church, including the institution of the observance of Sunday as a day of rest and worship, the emancipation of slaves, and new civil protections for Christians and Jews. The extent to which the new toleration ushered in by Constantine carried

25. Eusebius of Caesarea, *Vita Constantini*, bk. 2, pp. 30–41.

over outside the bounds of the empire is not, however, easy to document. Certainly it was a happy time for the community in Edessa, which reordered and better established itself, as we know from the *Chronicle of Edessa*, which records the ministries of nine bishops of that city during the fourth century. Circumstances were certainly less favorable in the Persian Empire under the reign of Shapur II (309–79), during which the Church of the East suffered heavy persecution and Nisibis came under Persian control in 363, resulting in the already discussed emigration of Ephrem, and many other Christians, to more tolerant Edessa. The Persian persecution did not spare the catholicos of Seleucia-Ctesiphon, Shimun Bar Sabbae, who was martyred on Good Friday in 341, along with a great many of his priests and monks, and the faithful. The next two catholicoi, Shahdost and Barba'shmin, suffered the same fate; and the persecution continued through the reign of Yazdegerd I (ending in 399)[26] and that of his son Bahram V, until 422, when the Roman Empire brought in tolerance for the cult of Zoroastrianism and the Persian Empire finally allowed Christian worship.

During this same period, the Christian communities of Mesopotamia suffered through the internal conflicts which plagued the wider Church in the form of the great theological and philosophical heresies of the time (Arianism, Novatianism, Adoptionism, Gnosticism, Sabellianism, and Nestorianism), and which led the universal Church to celebrate the four great ecumenical councils of Nicaea (325), Constantinople (381), Ephesus (431), and Chalcedon (451).

For the major doctrinal battle against the heresy of Arius (256–336),[27] which was undermining the Apostolic faith of Christ

26. See Mar Bawai Soro, "The Rise of Eastern Churches and Their Heritage 5th–8th Century—Churches of Syriac Tradition II, The Assyrian (East Syriacs)," in *Christianity: A History in the Middle East*, ed. Habib Badr (Beirut, Lebanon: Oikoumene, 2005), 255–87.

27. Arius, a priest of Alexandria, who was educated in Antioch, taught

as it had traditionally been believed and preached, the Emperor Constantine convoked the Council of Nicaea in May of 325. This included more than three hundred bishops, mostly from the Eastern Roman Empire, in an attempt to bring doctrinal and religious harmony to the Church and also to decide, among other matters, how to calculate and celebrate Easter as the principle feast of the Church.[28] The Nicene Creed affirmed the Church's faith in the divinity of Christ, but did not put an end to the Christological controversy, which later expanded to include the denial of the personhood and divinity of the Holy Spirit. The Emperor Theodosius I (379–95) subsequently convened another council in Constantinople, which confirmed the divinity of both the Son and the Holy Spirit, and the doctrine of the Trinity; it also recognized the primacy of the bishop of Rome, and assigned a position of honor to the patriarch of Constantinople (as the new Rome) among the other patriarchs.

Fifty years after the controversy over the Nicene Christology, a new debate surfaced over the Marian title "Mother of God" (*Theotokos*), which was already being used by prominent theologians and some of the faithful. The polemic exchange on this subject between Nestorius, bishop of Constantinople (428–31), and Cyril, bishop of Alexandria (412–44), deeply scarred the faith of the Eastern Church, even to this day. Nestorius advanced the concept of Mary as *Christotòkos* (which recognizes her as the mother of Jesus in his humanity, but not the Mother of God); Cyril squarely defended the title of Mary as *Theotokos* (Mother of

that Christ, as the Son of God, could not be considered the same as the Father nor coeternal with the Father, and was necessarily subordinate to the Father. His doctrine was formally condemned at Nicaea.

28. The Council of Nicaea was the first council after that of Jerusalem in the Apostolic age; it established, among other things, that Easter was to be celebrated on the first Sunday after the full moon after the spring equinox; that the ordination of a bishop was to happen with the participation of three other bishops and the confirmation of the metropolitan; and, finally, the primacy of the bishop of Rome over all the bishops of the Church.

God). The Council of Ephesus confirmed the doctrine of Mary's human-divine motherhood, as advocated by Cyril, and this was confirmed and validated by Pope Celestine (bishop of Rome). Twenty years later, again in response to burning controversies, the fourth great council was called, this time at Chalcedon, on the Bosphorus. The event was preceded by the so-called Robber Council of Ephesus, an assembly of bishops convened in 449 by the Emperor Theodosius II in defense of Eutyches and his Mono-physite doctrines, which were condemned by Pope Leo I (440–61). Chalcedon confirmed, under the direction of Pope Leo, the doctrine of the true faith in Jesus Christ as both truly God and truly man. This, in principle, reconstituted the unification of the Church in the East and West. For about 130 years, these doctrinal questions had troubled the Church and would continue to be a source of some contention for a long time to come.

At Nicaea, we know who attended the council, with James, bishop of Nisibis, and Saades, bishop of Edessa, both mentioned and who signed on behalf of the orthodoxy of the faithful of the church of Mesopotamia, which was also recognized as a metro-politan; similarly Eulogio (†386) is recorded as having attended the Council of Constantinople as metropolitan of Osroene.

The schools of Edessa and Nisibis, as the closest parts of Syria, and being strategically located on the way to Armenia, Anatolia, and Persia, suffered a considerable amount of turmoil through these doctrinal disputes. Rabbula, bishop of Edessa (412–35),[29] was opposed to the Nestorian doctrine and broke communion with Theodore of Mopsuestia (350–428), who had been his friend but who preached a dangerously unorthodox Christology;[30] Rab-

29. Rabbula was the son of a pagan and a Christian. He converted to Christianity in about the year 400, becoming first a monk and then bishop. He was initially hostile to Cyril of Alexandria and favored of Nestorius and Theodore of Mopsuestia, but after the Council of Ephesus (431), he strongly supported the conciliar doctrines.

30. Diodorus of Tarsus and Theodore of Mopsuestia were both teach-

bula then had Theodore, his ideas, and his writings condemned, and drove him and all of his supporters out of the Edessa School. Rabbula's efforts to keep the school doctrinally orthodox were somewhat undone by his successor, Hiba, bishop first from 435 to 449 and then from 451 until his death in 457, who, although not Nestorian, was close enough in some of his thoughts that he was deposed, to be later rehabilitated. It was through Hiba that the thought of Theodore of Mopsuestia came to be spread throughout the Eastern Church. The School of Edessa continued to be a place of controversy under Narsai, Hiba's successor as teacher in the school. Narsai fought with Cyrus, the bishop of Edessa from 471 to 498, and finally left the city when the school was closed by the Byzantine emperor Zeno in 489. Following this, first Narsai and then all the pro-Nestorians took refuge in Nisibis, then in Persian territory. Here Narsai, with the help of the bishop, Bar Sauma, reestablished the School of Nisibis, at which Nestorianism found a home.

Persia, which was politically opposed to Byzantium, deliberately cultivated an unorthodox Christianity, and the school at Nisibis formed generations of Nestorian theologians and clergy. Bar Sauma, bishop of Nisibis (460–84), a former student of the School of Edessa, had stirred up Nestorian opposition to Catholicos Babowai I of Seleucia-Ctesiphon, who was accused of being pro-Byzantium because of his orthodoxy, and who was executed in 484. The Nestorian Bar Sauma, who replaced Babowai in the See of Seleucia-Ctesiphon, formalized the ecclesial rupture with the Orthodox Churches and started the self-imposed mar-

---

ers of the Nestorian doctrine who died before it was declared dangerous and condemned. For Theodore of Mopsuestia the humanity assumed by the Word was a complete humanity, composed of rational soul and human flesh, so the Word was united to this humanity by grace. The Word, therefore, dwelt in this man as in a tent or in a temple. This union is not substantial presence, but simply of benevolence. From this it follows that Mary would be "antropotòkos" by nature and "Theotòkos" only by relationship. Nestorius substantially maintained the same doctrine as Theodore.

ginalization of the Church of the East. Bar Sauma was eventually murdered in 491 by opponents of the changes he brought in through the Synod of Beit Lapat (484),[31] when Nestorianism was declared doctrine for the Persian church, and which abolished ecclesiastical celibacy for monks and bishops. During this time, Seleucia-Ctesiphon, under Catholicos Mar Babai I (497–503), increasingly aligned the Church of the East with the Nestorian heresy; a synod authorized by the Sassanid King Djamasp confirmed the abolition of celibacy for all clergy and monastics and declared independence from other churches (497).[32] As a result of political pressures and the influence of renegade theologians, the Eastern Church had effectively become "Nestorian." This is not to say that its doctrines were welcomed by the faithful as theological truth; it seems more likely that it was the ongoing conflict between the Sassanid Empire, which sponsored Nestorianism, and the Eastern Roman Empire which weighed more heavily with the people. Political expediency and state support came to tell against doctrinal orthodoxy, and the prospect of a measure of internal peace would have been attractive to a Christian community exhausted by war and theological controversy. When we consider the appeal of the Nestorian cause, we must also take significant account of the emotive autonomy from the churches of Syria, Antioch, and Constantinople, that it offered the Eastern Church. This was always a strongly felt issue in the region: recall that, as early as 280, the metropolitan of Seleucia-Ctesiphon (Bar Aggai) had assumed the title of catholicos for himself and

31. Beit Lapat, in Persia, was founded by Shapur I, in about the year 260, to accommodate the prisoners sent there following military victories against the Byzantines; among them there were many Christians who began what would become an important community. Initially a diocese, Beit Lapat became metropolitan see of the Church of the East in 410.

32. Pablo Gefaell, "Las Iglesias orientales antiguas ortodoxas y católicas," in *Las Iglesias orientales*, ed. Adolfo González Montes (Madrid: Biblioteca de Autores Christiana, 2000), 607. Mar Babai I was married when he became patriarch.

his successors, and, by the synod of 410, "Grand Metropolitan and Primate of the Church of the East" had been added to the title. In fact, politics strongly favored separation and rewarded those who advanced its cause; in 424, Mar Dadisho I (421–56) assumed the title of patriarch. Yet, for all this, some scholars still believe that, despite the ascendance of Nestorianism in the Eastern Church, that faith professed during its synods of the fifth and sixth centuries was still largely orthodox, since the teachings of Nestorius only begin to appear in the records around 612. In essence, the Eastern Church would continue to adhere to orthodoxy, while the Sassanids kept her politically isolated and championed Nestorianism.[33] From its foundation until the Synod of Markabta, in 424, the seat of Seleucia-Ctesiphon had been led by twenty metropolitans; at that synod, it was announced that the catholicos could not be judged except by Christ himself, thus formalizing the independence from other Christian churches, even though the Church of the East had accepted the canons of the Council of Sardica (343), which stated the principle of the appeal to the pope in Rome in matters relating to bishops.[34]

In the fifth and sixth centuries, through alternating periods of persecution[35] and tolerance, the Church of the East endured considerable hardship during the wars between the Sassanids and the Byzantines, which served to make it an increasingly closed community. For 130 years, Mesopotamia, Syria (captured by Khosrow II in 611), Jerusalem (plundered and destroyed in 614), and even Egypt (621) were the scenes of military campaigns by the Persians. The retaliatory Byzantine campaign of 628 struck

33. See L. Sako, *The Chaldean Church—A Story of Being* (Kirkuk, Iraq: 2009), 7.

34. See Sacred Congregation for the Eastern Churches, *Oriente Cattolico —Cenni storici e statistiche* (Città del Vaticano: Sacra congregazione per le chiese orientali, 1974), 378.

35. In particular under Khosrow II, who tried to replace Christianity with a reversion to the pagan worship of a sun god.

deep into the heart of Mesopotamia, with the invasion reaching Nineveh and the plain of the Tigris as far as Ctesiphon. It was the beginning of the end of the Sassanids, who disappeared shortly after the invasion of Islamic Arabs and the killing of the last emperor, Yazdegerd III, at Merv in 651. In five short years of fighting between Arabs and Sassanids, the fall of the Persian Empire was rapid, and its territories were annexed by the caliphate.

From all this, these two centuries (the fifth and sixth), were crucial to the development of the missionary Church of the East, thanks to its monasticism, which came to benefit the entirety of Mesopotamia, Persia, Arabia and the coast to the north, and even the tribes of central Asia along the Silk Road. Monastic life, which still had a distinct Syrian influence, had become popular gradually in Upper Mesopotamia. Its beginnings near Nisibis are first recorded along with the hermit Yacoub in the late third century; he later became bishop of Nisibis, where he died in 338. Meanwhile, Edessa and Osroene had the monk Julian Mar Saba "the Elder" (†367), who attracted dozens of hermits. Both were the places where monastic communities formed and thrived, but the religious life there was probably not very disciplined, which led Rabbula, as bishop of Edessa, to try to develop a more regular system. Nevertheless, the monasteries, hermitages, and caves were frequented by men sincerely in search of God and a life of prayer and penance; and they were held in high esteem. Around the year 350, an important monastery was founded on Mount Izla, near Nisibis, from which monks spread out to other areas, founding new monasteries as they went. Of particular note is the beginning of hermit life among women; Theodoret[36] remembers two, Marana and Cira, who created monasteries for themselves and for other women, where they lived a retired life. Ephrem the Syrian mentions the "Daughters of the Covenant," in Nisibis: Plotinide, Tomaide and Febronia; the last of whom

36. Theodoret was the last great theologian of the School of Antioch, a

was a great spiritual guide for her sisters and was martyred under Diocletian (†305). It is also worth noting that Rabbula, who was bishop at the time, mentions the presence of deaconesses who lived as a recluses, either attached to a church or with their own families. This reality continued to evolve, during the fifth and sixth centuries, into new forms of community life.

Yet the fifth century also saw the contamination of the monastic life of the Church of the East by the decision of the Synod of Beit Lapat to abolish celibacy for monks; this provision caused enormous tensions until its eventual revision in 553. While it was Abraham Kashkar (492–586), abbot of the monastery of Mount Izla, who served as the great reformer against the abolition of celibacy, it was Patriarch Babai the Great (609–28) who actually carried out the reforms, systematically expelling all the married monks from the monasteries. The reforming movement gave the monks a true missionary function through the establishment of monasteries in the places to be evangelized, and it also saw the founding of monasteries as centers of theological knowledge and priestly formation to meet the increasingly urgent needs of the Church. From these houses of learning, numerous monks were called to lead dioceses. Under Patriarch Aba I (540–52), the Church of the East was reorganized and, by the time of Babai the Great, himself a monk from Mount Izla, the people of Mesopotamia and Persia were largely Christian. By the time of the Arab conquest (651) the Church of the East had spread as far as China, with the Christian faith professed in Kumbaliq, in modern Uzbekistan, and episcopal sees established in Afghanistan (Herat), Samarkand (Uzbekistan), and India.

---

zealous bishop of Cyrus and a champion against the Monophysitism of Eutyches. He was born in about 393 and died around 466. In addition to numerous theological writings, he produced a history of monasticism (440) and an ecclesiastical history (450) in continuation with that of Eusebius, as well as an abbreviated history of the heresies (453).

Chapter 2

The Church of the East

The Arab (651–1258), Mongol (1258–1410),
and Turkish (1410–1508) Ages

1. The Arab Conquest and Occupation, and the Expansion of the Church of the East: Glory and Decline

Just a decade after the Hegira in 622 AD,[1] the Arabs struck out from the Arabian Peninsula and began their conquest of Egypt, Palestine, and Syria, attacking first Byzantium and then the Persians, who were defeated at al-Qadisiyah (637). They took Ctesiphon, the capital of their empire, and forced open the way to the east, toward the interior of central Persia. Within a few short years, the territory stretching from of the middle of Byzantium and across the Persian Empire was in their hands and integrated into the caliphate. Both empires had been steadily weakening each other through repeated wars, while the Byzantine suppression of the Monophysites, together with other doctrinal and political struggles, had left the Christian state constitutionally fragile, and its people easily subdued by the invaders. Adapting to their new circumstances cannot have been easy; while the Christian population was not made to forcibly convert to Islam, as subjects of the caliphate they were forced to pay a special protection tax (jizya), which replaced the already heavy and hated

1. Muhammed's departure from Mecca to Medina.

taxes of the Sassanians. This arrangement did nothing to stop anti-Christian actions by Arab administrators, for whom it was a simple matter of fact that "the faithful" (Muslims) could not be considered equal to "infidels," be they Christian or otherwise. For a non-Muslim conquered by an Islamic people through *jihad*, there is a simple "free" choice between conversion, death, slavery, or, for a Christian or Jew, the status of *dhimmi*, that is a "protected" person by virtue of their payment of a special tax provided for by the Pact of Umar.[2]

The old Christian provinces, both Roman and Sassanian, with their important religious and cultural cities, did their best to adapt to the new reality. Exercising a certain political pragmatism, the conquerors sought to strike terms with the occupied Christian tribes and towns, offering them freedom of worship and a measure of self-administration, and typically leaving the current system intact as much as possible. Through its historical origins, Islam had acquired many of its basic elements from the Judeo-Christian faith, including the oneness of God, the importance of Jesus (their understanding of whom was heavily influenced by Nestorianism) and of the figure of Mary. Some aspects of Islamic moral and spiritual life (prayer five times a day, fasting, almsgiving) also seem to have been borrowed from Christianity. This meant that the Muslim invaders had some tolerance for the Christians whom they now ruled. As a result, the religious life of the Christian community was not immediately subjected to total upheaval—churches, and even monasteries, continued to enjoy a certain freedom. This did not last long. Simple economic pressure led many of the poorest and weakest, who could not afford to pay the *jizya* and maintain their protected status, to choose to convert to Islam. Other

2. The Pact of Umar is an historical treatise attributed to the Caliph Umar ibn al-Khattab (637). It regulates the civil status and relationships of non-Muslims (Christians and Jews) in the lands conquered by Islamic people.

conversions to the religion of the conquerors took place as part of matrimonial alliances formed when a Christian married a Muslim; others were motivated by longstanding feuds, jealousy, or political calculation. There were even cases of whole tribes in southern-central Mesopotamia converting to Islam for political and economic interests and opportunities, as was the case of the Nestorian Lakhmids of al-Hirah, who had first been evangelized by the monks of Church of the East. Even the Zoroastrians of Persia abandoned their religion, almost *en masse*, for Islam.

In the patristic Christian world, the Arab conquest was seen only in negative terms. This was reflected in the writings of many, including Sophronius, a theologian-monk, strong defender of orthodoxy, and bishop of Jerusalem (634–38), who saw the city succumb to the Arabs in 638, but who persuaded the Caliph Umar to enter the Holy City as a pilgrim, rather than a conqueror. Maximus the Confessor (580–662), another monk and theologian, in one of his letters from Alexandria (Letter 14), denounced the caliphate's policies as cruelty in the name of God. John of Damascus (650–749), the last great theologian of the Greek Church, the son of the civil head of the Christian population of the Caliphate of Damascus, polemicist scourge of the Nestorians, Monophysites,[3] Monothelites,[4] and Manichaeans,[5] called Islam the "101st heresy" and bluntly repudiated every aspect of the Muslim faith. His successive apologetics served to defend the Christian faith against the new religion of the invaders, and simultaneously helped to develop an extraordinary lit-

---

3. The monophysite heresy asserted that Christ had only one nature, that of the Word, which was merely clad in human flesh. The Monophysites of Egypt, resentful of the orthodox doctrines enforced by Constantinople, welcomed the Arab invasion as a means of freeing themselves from Constantinople's control.

4. These held that there was only one will, the Divine, in Christ.

5. The Manichaeans held to a cosmic dualism, in which good and evil were locked in eternal struggle.

erary movement[6] which introduced classical Greek thought into the Muslim world, including medicine, mathematics, and art. In this way he started a great cultural current that would shape the Church of the East, together with the other churches under Arab rule.

Mesopotamia—with its historical schools (Edessa, Nisibis) and the fervor of its new demographic and cultural centers, such as Baghdad, under the influence of the Abbasids—once more became a beacon of civilization, recalling its ancient glories. The Arabs became the vehicle of this culture, first linguistically, and then in all aspects of life: religious, administrative, educational, and philosophical. This caused Islamic thought to undergo an impressive evolution, with Koranic exegesis, born out of Christian methodology, developing within the Islamic canon, inspiring new philosophical, mystical, theological, and philological traditions, as well as a hunger for scientific knowledge, architecture, and art.

Christian thought in the eighth through eleventh centuries was a field crowded with impressive names. Without going into excessive detail, it is worth cataloging those who made a series of contributions and who merit special mention as important figures: Timothy I, catholicos of the Church of the East, who lived from 728 to 823 and who was the protagonist of a fascinating debate with the Caliph al-Mahdi; the Nestorian Abu ibn al-Salt al-Ambari, a contemporary of Timothy's and almost equally influential in his writings, especially for his rejection of the Qur'an, and his writings on the unity of God and the doctrine of the Trinity; Theodore Abu Qurrah of Edessa (750–820), the Melkite theologian, bishop of Harran, and author of numerous treatises, in both Arabic and Greek, defending first orthodoxy

6. See I. M. Beaumont, *Christology in Dialogue with Muslims: A Critical Analysis of Christian Presentations of Christ for Muslims from the Ninth and Twentieth Centuries* (Oregon: Regnum, 2005).

against the Monophysites and Nestorians, and later the Christian faith against the Muslims; Abu Raita al-Takriti (†830), who was the author of four major theological treatises and a letter on the Trinity, addressed to a Muslim, explaining the mystery of the Trinity, as well as a similar letter on the Incarnation; Ammar al-Basri (who lived around 800–850) a Nestorian and native of Basra, who wrote two apologias in Arabic; Hunayn ibn Ishaq (808–73), another Nestorian, who wrote about how to identify true religion and illustrated how Christianity corresponds to all such criteria; his son Ishaq was himself an important translator and writer; Abd al-Masih ibn Ishaq al-Kindi, who lived in the late ninth and early tenth centuries, was a polemicist who wrote a dialogue between a Muslim and a Christian, with each calling upon the other to convert; Yahya ibn 'Adi (†974) was a Syriac-Jacobite, a philosopher, theologian, and polemicist, as well as a translator of Plato and Aristotle; Issa ibn Zurah (†1008) was an apologist, doctor, and philosopher living in Baghdad; Nasr Abu Yahya ibn Jarir (c. 1030–1103), a Syriac-Jacobite priest, worked and wrote as a physician, astronomer, and theologian; Elias of Nisibis (c. 1049) was metropolitan of that city and a Nestorian theologian who wrote an account of seven meetings he had with the vizier al-Maghribi; Abdallah Ibn al-Tayyib (1000–1050), a Nestorian, physician, and commentator on Greek classics, a prolific writer as a biblical scholar and theologian; and Gewargis Wardā, the Nestorian hymnographer of Arbil, who lived toward the end of the twelfth century.

In the ongoing theological dispute between Muslims and Christians, special mention should be made of the efforts of the Caliph al-Ma'mun, who governed the Umma (the worldwide Islamic community) between 813 and 833 and who founded the Bayt al-Hikma (House of Wisdom) in Baghdad; this was a meeting place for the Islamic scholars and translators of the caliphate that gathered, honed, and disseminated ideological instruments to be used against the "infidels" which focused especially on the—as he called it—"irrationality" of Christianity and which made Islam the true successor to Greek thought.

In this context, it should be remembered that, first under the Umayyads (661–750) and then the Abbasids (750–1258), there were notable instances of conversion to Islam from among the faithful of the Eastern Church. These episodes were driven by a variety of factors including: the extent to which Christianity was rooted (or not) in the population; the jihadist vocation of Islam; the penalized legal condition of Christians; and the imposition of economic and administrative rules, such as the adoption of Arabic as the official language of public administration,[7] which saw the replacement of Christian governors and administrators with Muslims, and Persian ones with Arabs. At the social level, this produced significant consequences in Christian communities, which, while isolating them, formed the basis for their own cultural preservation through the continued use of their own spoken language (Syriac-Aramaic), the closure of villages to non-Christians, and the protection of their lands through conscious intermarriage between Christians. The Arabic language was, in turn, used mainly for dealings with outsiders and for business contracts. After the destruction of Seleucia-Ctesiphon (642), the patriarchal seat of the Church of the East had to be moved, and its missionary activity in Mesopotamia lost direction and impetus, ironically just at the time it was making great advances outside the Arab territories.[8]

During this early period the Church of the East was led by a number of influential and important catholicos, such as Ishoyahb II (628–45), who established the order of precedence of

7. This was brought in under Caliph al-Walid (705–15), the third of the Umayyad dynasty.

8. Under Catholicos Ishoyahb II (628–45) the patriarchal seat was moved to the city of Kirkuk.

the episcopal sees during the synod of 642;[9] Maremmeh (647–49), who studied at Nisibis and was a virtuous and charitable monk; and Ishoyahb III (650–58), also educated at Nisibis, who was first a monk and then later bishop of Nineveh, metropolitan of Adiabene, and finally catholicos of the Church of the East. Ishoyahb III was able to keep good relations with the Arabs, strengthened his primatial role, and reformed the liturgy; he was responsible for the selection of three anaphoras for the Eucharistic celebration, known by the names of "Addai and Mari," "Theodore," and "Nestorius"; and, with the help of the monk Henanisho, he oversaw the final drafting of choral *Hudra* (cycle for liturgical service).[10]

It was during the tenure of the two subsequent catholicoi (Giwargis I and Yohannan I) that Islam underwent its greatest schism, following the assassination of al-Husain ibn Ali, who was killed at Karbala in 680. His followers, as opposed to the Sunni Umayyads (661–759), created the Shiite branch of Islam around their strongholds in the sacred cities of Karbala and Najaf. Shiism would become the predominant Islamic faith in lower Mesopotamia, and from there it spread into Persia. Following the revolt of the Abbasids eighty years later, the caliphate was moved from Damascus to Baghdad (762),[11] which became the new capital and the seat of the catholicate of the Church of the East under Timothy I. In this unified geopolitical context, Islamic persecution of Christians abated, and the Church of the East began to spread westward, creating episcopal sees in Damascus, Jerusalem, and Alexandria. Meanwhile, on the Asian subcontinent, and even in some the most central areas of Asia,

9. The order of precedence of the sees put forward by the metropolitan was: Beit Lapat (Gundishapur), Nisibis, Basra, Arbil, Kirkuk, Rawardashir, Merv, and Halah.

10. See L. Sako, *The Chaldean Church—A Story of Being* (Kirkuk, Iraq: 2009), 10.

11. Founded by the Caliph al-Mansur between 762 and 767.

missions were established as far away as Tibet. Writing in 1318, the Syriac chronicler Abdisho of Nisibis records that the Church of the East had, by his time, grown to include twenty metropolitan sees and two hundred bishoprics.

The line of the catholicos, from the transfer of the headquarters to Baghdad (775) until the schism in the Church of the East (1552), enumerates forty-six patriarchs, whose patriarchal sees were not in Mesopotamia; under Patriarch Mar Yahballaha III (1281–1317),[12] the see moved again, this time to Maragha, in the northwest section of present-day Iran, not far from Lake Urmia, a city built by the Mongol Hulagu Khan (1217–65).[13] It was Hulagu Khan who sacked Baghdad on February 13, 1258. This event, which included the tragic ruin of its extraordinary library, rich in valuable historical texts, left the city a shattered ruin, uninhabited for many years.

2. The Mongol and Turkish Period; the Church of the East Approaches Rome

The history of Patriarch Yahballaha III's reign is intertwined with the Church of Rome. It is an interesting period as it is one of the first moments of contact between the Church of the East

12. Mar Yahballaha III was born Rabban Markos at Beijing in 1245 and is believed to have been of Turkish-Uyghur descent. He undertook a pilgrimage from China to Jerusalem with his traveling companion, Rabban Bar Sauma. During the pilgrimage Rabban Markos met the Patriarch Mar Dinkha I (1265–81), who appointed him metropolitan of China; but following Dinkha's death, before he could return there, Rabban Markos was elected as his successor as Patriarch of the Church of the East and took the name of Yahballaha III (1281–1317). Very probably his election was due to the influence it was thought he could wield with the Mongols. In 1304 he went to reside at Maragha, the Mongol capital, where he remained for the rest of his life.

13. Hugalu Khan was a grandson of Genghis Khan and a brother of Kublai Khan. His mother was a Nestorian Christian of the Church of the East, as was his wife, though he was himself a Buddhist.

and the supreme authority of the Church of Rome, after centuries of isolation. It began when Rabban Bar Sauma was sent to the West, on the patriarch's behalf, to seek an audience with the pope, and to act as the Mongols' ambassador to the courts of Philip IV of France and Edward I of England.[14] The recently elected Franciscan, Pope Nicholas IV (1288–92), was eager to greet him, presenting him with numerous gifts for the patriarch, including the papal ring, and a bull recognizing Yahballaha as "Patriarch of all the Christians of the East." Bar Sauma himself received Communion from the pope's hand on Palm Sunday in 1288, and was granted faculties to celebrate the Eucharist.[15] In Rome, Bar Sauma was himself a possible flashpoint between the Western Church and the Church of the East, which did not use the *Filioque* in the Creed. Nicholas IV was not unaware of the tension; as a monk, he had been part of the papal delegation sent to invite Greek delegates to the Council of Lyons in 1276. Because of this sensitivity, he ensured that Bar Sauma was paid every courtly attention and courtesy. Nicholas IV was a pious man and a lover of peace, where the good of the Church was concerned. He was also deeply interested in the fate of the Holy Land and its liberation, and in doing what he could for the missions among the Tartars and the Chinese. It was his hope that establishing cordial relations with the Church of the East would be to the common benefit of the wider Christian cause. Patriarch Yahballaha responded warmly to these overtures and, in a letter addressed to Benedict XI (1303–4) in May of 1304, he made his profession of faith; sadly his intended union with Rome was rejected by the Nestorian bishops. As for Bar Sauma, he returned to Baghdad, where he wrote his memoirs and died in 1294.

14. Bar Sauma was born around 1220 at Beijing and was of Uyghur decent; a monk at twenty, he instructed Rabban Markos as a student.

15. This was granted despite some controversy over his failure to mention the *Filioque* in the Creed: "I have not come here to disagree," he is said to have told the cardinals, "but to venerate the pope."

With the end of the Abbasid dynasty (1258), the Church of the East had a brief period of peace; various Mongol leaders, including Kublai Khan, had Christian mothers, the *jizya* was abolished, and Christians were again allowed to serve in higher governmental positions. Historic cities, dear to Christianity, passed from Arab hands into Mongol control (Nisibis, Edessa, Aleppo and Damascus), but peace did not last long. After the death of Kublai Khan (1294), the Mongol Ghazan Khan (1271–1304), though born to a Christian mother and instructed in Buddhism, converted to Islam when he ascended the throne in 1295 and immediately began attacking the Christian community, reintroducing the *jizya* while destroying many churches, or ordering them converted into mosques. The Christians who had so recently enjoyed a measure of freedom, were suddenly once again the target of Muslim persecution and violence. For about a century, the Church of the East saw many of its churches and monasteries destroyed; and, under the thirty-year reign of Ghazan, there was a Christian exodus from cities like Baghdad, Tikrit, Kirkuk, and Arbil. This period of renewed persecution was given terrible punctuation by two massacres of Christians in Arbil (1310) and Amid (1317); these included the killing of women and children, with the survivors reduced to slavery. The dispersion of Christians left a deep mark upon the religious geography of central and southern Mesopotamia, brought to completion by Tamerlane (1336–1405), a fierce Mongolian Turk, who led his hordes to sack Baghdad, first in 1393, and then a second time in 1401 when, it is said, his men massacred ninety thousand people, Christian and Sunni. After that, Baghdad was reduced to a mere provincial city.[16]

Yahballaha III was succeeded as patriarch by Timothy II (1318–31), who celebrated what was to be the last of the synods of

---

16. See D. Wilmshurst, *The Ecclesiastical Organization of the Church of the East 1318–1913* (Leuven: Peeters, 2000), 185.

the Church of the East until the nineteenth century. During the long reign of Tamerlane, most of the Church of the East was destroyed; and Christian communities from Persia to China were cut off from the mother Church, disappearing after 1368. Christian expansion in the East came to a jarring halt, as it did in Mesopotamia where the population was decimated, stalked by strife, hunger, and terrible diseases like the plague. The patriarchal see was continually moved to whatever place could offer the catholicos a measure of security; Patriarch Dinkha II (1336–81) had his see first in Karamles, on the Plain of Nineveh, and then moved to Qodchanis, in the Kurdish mountains of Hakkari, an isolated region unconnected to the most important transport routes.

Under Shimon Basidia IV (1437–97), there was a new rapprochement between Rome and the Church of the East during the Council of Florence in 1445, when Pope Eugene IV issued the bull *Benedictus sit Deus* (August 7, 1445), on union with the Chaldean of Cyprus; its use of the word "Chaldean" referred specifically to the Nestorians in communion with Rome:

Blessed be God, ... that accompanies the growing, with many and great signs of benevolence and outcome happier than we deserve, ... union of the Eastern Church with the Western in the Ecumenical Council of Florence, after the Armenians, the Jacobites and peoples of Mesopotamia were brought back to obedience ... , the Chaldeans sent down to us Timothy, their Metropolitan, (who) first, with reverence and devotion, he made his solemn profession of faith and doctrine ... in this way: I, Timothy, Archbishop of Tarsus, Metropolitan of Cyprus of the Chaldeans, promise for myself and all my peoples ... before you, blessed father, Eugene IV, most holy Pope, and this Apostolic See ... that in the future I will always be under obedience to you, your successors, and the holy Roman Church, as the only mother and head of all the others.[17]

17. Pope Eugene IV, bull *Benedictus sit Deus*, 14, August 7, 1445. Cf. inter alia, S. Rassam, *Christianity in Iraq* (Melbourne, Australia: Freedom Publishing, 2010), 108.

3. Schism in the Church of the East; the Chaldean Church

While this union with Rome was extremely short-lived, it was not an isolated incident. Eventual lasting communion with Rome came as a result of a schism within the Church of the East itself. This was precipitated by the decision of Patriarch Shimon Basidia IV, taken with the apparent aim of insulating the position from interference by the Turkish-Islamic authorities,[18] to declare that his office would now be a hereditary prerogative of his family, descending from uncle to nephew. He was succeeded by four patriarchs: Shimon V (1497–1501), Eliya V (1502–3), Shimon VI (1504–38) and Shimon Bar Mama Ishoyahb VII (1539–58).[19] Throughout the ministries of each of these, the controversy caused by the establishment of a hereditary line never abated, with various bishops demanding a return to the elective practice.[20] After years of arguing, these bishops elected a patriarch of their own in 1552, Yohannan Sulaqa, abbot of the Rabban Hormizd monastery at Alqosh. When he and his election were denounced and he was called an antipatriarch, he turned to the pope for recognition. Sulaqa, using the Franciscans as intermediaries, went to Rome, where he appeared before Julius III and professed the Catholic faith on February 20, 1553. Julius ordained him bishop and gave him the pallium and the title of Patriarch of Mosul and Assyria,[21] this was then changed, almost immediately, to Patriarch of the Chaldeans. Sulaqa then returned to Amid (Diyarbekir), taking the patriarchal name Shimon VIII Yohannan

18. After Tamerlane, Iraq was ruled by two Turkish factions until the Persian Safavid dynasty displaced them by their occupation of Mesopotamia in 1508; they, in turn, were replaced by the Ottomans in 1538.

19. Shimon VII, to the great scandal of the faithful, consecrated two of his nephews as metropolitans, one of whom was twelve years old at the time, and the other fifteen.

20. This resistance was led by the bishops of Amid, Sert, and Urmia.

21. In Rome it was believed that Patriarch Shimon VII had died.

Sulaqa (1553–55), accompanied by two Dominicans tasked with teaching the Catholic faith.[22]

The new patriarch then ordained two metropolitans and three bishops, but at the instigation of the Nestorian Shimon VII, the Ottomans arrested, tortured, and killed him in 1555; and he is now considered a martyr of the union with Rome. The bishops consecrated by Sulaqa then elected, as his successor, Abdisho IV Maron (1555–70), who received recognition by Pope Pius IV in 1562, and who resided at the monastery at Seert. From Sulaqa, there extends a patriarchal line, known as Shimon Line, which had several residences (Amid, Seert, Urmia, Salmas); though not all the successors of Sulaqa obtained papal recognition by going to Rome or by profession of faith. After Abdisho IV Maron, there were three patriarchs: Yaballaha V Shimon (1572–80); Shimon IX Dinkha (1580–1600), last to be formally recognized by Rome and who reintroduced hereditary succession; and Shimon X Eliya (1600–1638), who moved the patriarchal see to Salmas. Shimon X was succeeded by three further patriarchs, Shimon XI Eshuyow (1638–56), Shimon XII Yoalaha (1656–62), and Shimon XIII Dinkha (1662–1700), who went to reside in Qochanis and formally broke communion with Rome in 1692.

In Alqosh, meanwhile, there was the Eliya Line, so-called because of the name taken by patriarchs who lived there. Some consider this patriarchal line to be the original one, dating back to the Church of the East before her schism and even to St. Thomas himself. In this line there is Eliya VII (1558–91); Eliya VIII (1591–1617), who entered into communion with Rome, though this was repudiated by his successor, Eliya IX Shimon (1617–60); after these came Eliya X Marogin Yohannan (1660–1700) and four other patriarchs. In 1778, following the death of Eliya XII Dinkha, the patriarchy in Alqosh split between Eliya XIII Ishoyahb (1778–1804), who was not in communion with

22. Rassam, *Christianity in Iraq*, 109.

Rome, and his cousin Yohannan VIII Eliya Hormizd (1778–1830), who professed the Catholic faith upon the death of Eliya XIII. All of these patriarchs, who did not have automatic hereditary succession, were at the head of the largest patriarchal community.

In 1681, at Amid, a third patriarchal line was formed, called the Yousuf Line, when it separated from the seat of Alqosh and entered into communion with Rome. This occurred when Archbishop Yousuf Amid, under Capuchin influence, broke away from Patriarch Eliya X Yohannan Marogin (1660–1700), gaining recognition from the pope and taking the name of Yusuf I (1681–96); he was succeeded by three patriarchs, Yousuf II Sliba Maruf (1696–1713), Yousuf III Maroge Timothy (1713–57), and Yousuf IV Lazare Hindi (1757–80). These remained in communion with the Catholic Church as patriarchs until Yousuf V Augustine Hindi (1780–1827), who was the patriarchal administrator from 1802, and apostolic delegate to the See of Babylon of the Chaldeans from 1812. Augustine Hindi was never recognized by Rome as patriarch, and the seat remained formally vacant until 1830, when, with Patriarch Yohannan VIII Eliya Hormizd, the Eliya Line reunited with the Yousuf Line to constitute the current Chaldean Church based in Mosul.

In this complex history, the so-called Shimon line in Qochanis continued autonomously under a series of patriarchs taking that name, until the last, Shimon XXI Ishai (1920–75), with whom the practice of hereditary succession ended. This patriarchal line now forms the Assyrian Church of the East, which in 1964 endured its own schism, with the creation of the Ancient Church of the East.

From the twelfth century onward, the Church of the East, through all the historical events discussed, saw a rapid decline as it shrank not only geographically but numerically as well, becoming almost an ethno-religious identity, without territory, mostly focused on its own survival and a nostalgic yearning for the past glories of the sixth to twelfth centuries. This situation was compounded not only by the relative isolation in which the surviving community lived, but also by the encroachment of Islam, both religious and political, from the Mongol conquests through Ottoman rule, which ended with the genocide of Armenians, Assyrians, and Chaldeans in the early twentieth century. But the most delicate crisis originated and remained within the church itself through the chaos of patriarchal lines and successions; a lack of pastoral life among the clergy; conflict between episcopal sees, which became almost family feuds; lack of formation among the (mostly married) priesthood; and various crises of reform and counter-reform in religious life.

A significant boost was given to the recovery and pastoral renewal of this stream of Christianity through its contacts and relations with the Latin Church; first through the Franciscans, who worked very successfully in Upper Mesopotamia, and who led several bishops and many of the faithful to the Catholic communion, and then through the Dominicans, Carmelites, and Jesuits. These missionaries brought a lifeblood and spiritual energy to the Chaldean Church, organizing and supporting piety, religious life, and the educational training of the clergy and the people.

Chapter 3

The Latin Church in Mesopotamia

The Safavid Dynasty and the Ottoman Era

1. The Origins of the Latin Missions in Persia and Mesopotamia

For twenty-six years, from 1508 to 1534, the Persian dynasty of the Safavids occupied Mesopotamia, succeeding Turkic control. Shah Ismail I assumed power in Persia in 1487 and later, in 1502, declared Shiite Islam to be the state religion. When he took possession of the "land between two rivers" in 1508, the Sunni Ottoman-Turks were suitably alarmed, seeing the annexation of Mesopotamia as part of a politically and religiously expansionist Persian policy. Consequently, Sultan Selim I (1465–1520), who was himself a rather ruthless monarch, began a campaign against the Persians, eventually defeating them at Caldron in 1514; though it was Suleiman the Magnificent (1520–66) who eventually conquered Baghdad in 1534, and with it secured the surrender of most of Mesopotamia. From this point on, the region was a continuous battleground, especially from the borders of Anatolia as far as Baghdad and Basra, near to which lie the Shiite holy sites. The continuing conflict between the Persians and the Ottomans often made life difficult for missionaries who, in the sixteenth century, had begun to take an interest both in Persia and in Mesopotamia.

The history of the launch of the Latin Church's presence in Persia and Mesopotamia is a deeply interesting story: the paths of missionaries in these two countries intertwined for years as the first dioceses were created and the first provisions were made for episcopal appointments and the necessities of pastoral life. The presence of missionaries was an essential catalyst for the encounter between the Church of Rome and the Church of the East, an encounter which bore tangible fruit in origins of the Chaldean Church, and which helped carve a space for the vibrant Syriac-Catholic, Greek-Melkite, and Armenian-Catholic communities.

The Council of Trent, as part of its deliberations on the nature and focus of the post-Reformation Church, had recommended a renewed emphasis on missionary work, both in the territories of the Protestant Reformation and in the new lands which were rapidly opening up to the west and east of Europe. Particular attention was also to be paid to the Near East, which was the territory of the ancient Eastern Churches, where the invasive presence of Islam had spread and entrenched itself over nine centuries. In this region especially, Christian unity was an imperative, as was demonstrated when the Nestorian Catholicate, under Yohannan Sulaqa, entered into communion with Rome in 1553.

Before Trent, communication with the countries of the Levante had been sporadic. Generally, missionaries travelled across the lands of Mesopotamia northward, to meet the Silk Road and continue eastward; it was rare for anyone to turn south and descend along the Euphrates or the Tigris, or spend any time in the land bordered by the two major rivers. One of the first known Latin missionaries was the Frenchman Guillaume de Montferrat—disciple and companion of St. Dominic, founder of the Order of Preachers—who came to the court of the caliph of Baghdad in 1235. Some decades later, a Florentine Dominican named Ricoldo of Montecroce,[1] having received a mandate from Pope Nicholas IV to preach in the East, reached Mosul and then Baghdad in 1290. There Patriarch Yaballaha III extended to him the right to preach in the Nestorian Cathedral—though he clashed with the local clergy when he referred to "Mary, Mother of God" and spoke out against Nestorius. In spite of this, the Mongols gave him permission to construct an oratory, though not permission to evangelize. During his ten-year tenure there, he began his translation of the Qur'an into Latin, travelled extensively throughout the region, visited the local monasteries, and recorded his experiences in his *Book of a Pilgrimage in Parts of the East*. After him, until the fourteenth century, both Dominican preachers and Franciscan friars intermittently travelled through the region and secured relationships, though sometimes tenuous ones, between Rome and the Nestorian patriarchs.

To give impetus to the Council of Trent's expectations, ten years after its conclusion Pope Gregory XIII created the Congregation for Greek Affairs, in 1573, which was charged with the special care of Eastern Christians. This was then changed by Clement VIII to the Congregation on Matters of Faith and the Catholic Religion. It was, however, Pope Gregory XV who, with the constitution *Inscrutabili divinae* (1622), erected the Sacra Congregatio de Propaganda Fide (Sacred Congregation for the Propagation of the Faith), responsible for all the Church's missionary outreaches, and to which was entrusted the care of much of the Eastern Catholic missions. The congregation, which had the stated mission of propagating and defending the Catholic faith, was further reformed, shortly thereafter, by Urban VIII

1. Ricoldo of Montecroce (1243–1320) traveled through Asia Minor up to Mesopotamia between 1288 and 1300. His account is one of the first to tell the many "wonders" of the Near East and to describe the places and people he encountered (see Enrico Artifoni et al., *Storia medievale* [Rome: Donzelli Editore, 1998], 405).

(1623–44) who constituted two committees with special responsibility for meeting the pastoral needs of Eastern Christians and to promote the reunion of the Eastern Churches with Rome. At the same time, the pope founded the College for Propaganda Fide (1627), which was the first center for the education and training of indigenous priests, including those from Mesopotamia. Seeking to expand on the historical insight of Gregory XV, Pope Pius IX, in 1862, created the section Pro negotiis ritus orientalis within Propaganda Fide. This was expanded upon by Benedict XV in the great curial reforms of 1917, in which he created the current Congregation for Eastern Churches, in order to deepen the identity of the Eastern Churches, promote a better understanding of them and their organic union, and preserve their fellowship and diversity in ritual, discipline, and spirituality.

The establishment of a stable presence of the Latin Church in Mesopotamia is bound up with the events which led to the establishment of the Diocese of Baghdad, which was created on September 6, 1632, and which was interconnected, for nearly a century, with the Diocese of Isfahan, in Persia, established three years earlier on October 12, 1629. At this point in time, Persia was ruled, with an iron fist, by Shah Abbas I (1587–1629), who had extended his territory westward into Mesopotamia by conquest. During his reign, he had extensive correspondence with the popes in Rome. In a letter dated September 30, 1592, Clement VIII invited the shah to join the Christian League in its war against the Turkish Sultan, with whom the Persian king was already fighting; indeed, Abbas had a real incentive to maintain good relations with the West in order to weaken the increasingly powerful and warlike Ottoman Empire.

Communications were difficult. Missionaries and traders were almost the only ones willing to attempt a journey either along blocked roads or over dangerous seas, and, either way, trips were long and fraught with danger. Three barefoot religious brothers of the Order of St. Augustine managed one such journey; sent by the viceroy of the Portuguese Indies, they arrived in Persia by sea, reaching Isfahan sometime between May of 1603 and January of 1604. They constituted the first Catholic mission to settle in Persia with consent of the shah. These Augustinians were already in Isfahan when, in July 1607, the Discalced Carmelite father Paolo Simone di Gesù Maria arrived in Persia with a small group of religious and requested an audience with Shah Abbas. This small delegation of five Carmelites had been sent by Clement VIII and arrived in the Persian capital via Poland, Russia, and the Caucasus.

Their group included Fr. Juan Taddeo, who would become the first bishop of Isfahan. The group presented themselves to the shah as "emissaries of the pope" and were accepted in that capacity. Shah Abbas accorded them considerable diplomatic courtesy, suggesting the exchange of stable ambassadors between his empire and the papal court, even inviting Rome to appoint a bishop of Isfahan for the better assimilation of his Armenian Christian subjects.[2] This small Carmelite community, now under the shah's protection, threw themselves into their new surroundings, studying the local languages of Persian and Armenian, as well as the religious customs and traditions of the Armenians, among whom they began their missionary work. Unfortunately for them, the Augustinians did not enjoy such high favor at court; they finally left the city in 1613 and headed first to Baghdad, and then on to Basra. The Portuguese had commercial interests in both of these cities and were able to give the Augustinians a greater measure of protection in their work.

The primary objective of the Carmelites in Persia was to bring the schismatic Nestorians and Armenians back into commu-

2. *A Chronicle of the Carmelites in Persia and the Papal Mission of the XVIIth and XVIIIth Centuries*, vol. 1 (London: Eyre and Spottiswoode, 1939), 148.

nion with Rome and the Catholic faith, while having a pastoral concern for travelers coming through the territory on commercial business. They also had an interest in humanitarian work, with particular attention to the redemption of Christians who, for debts or other reasons, had been sold into slavery to wealthy Muslims.[3] Soon, Syrian Christians, Armenians, Georgians, Arabs, and Nestorians were all coming to the Carmelites for spiritual and moral support, though they abstained from direct missionary action when dealing with the Muslim population, which was totally prohibited. Urban VIII commended these intrepid missionaries to the benevolence of the shah as "Our children and delegates ... for the propagation of the faith in Basra of Babylon, and, as in Babylon, in Arabia also."[4] By 1623, the Carmelite mission in Basra had begun, almost unnoticed, with three priests and, in the same year, the first Mass in Persia was celebrated in Shiraz.

At this time, the political and economic interests of the European kingdoms were booming, and their missionary work was a necessary support to their wider ambitions. France looked toward the Persian Gulf, where the Portuguese, Spanish, Dutch, and English had already established themselves, thanks to the novel diplomatic strategy of force projection through gunboat diplomacy. Since they were already present in the Turkish Empire, in 1628 Cardinal Richelieu pushed the French Capuchins to go to Persia. On June 23, 1628, three religious left Aleppo, reaching Qazwin (north of Tehran) after twenty-five days of travel. One of these bore a letter from the king of France, credentialing him as the new ambassador to the shah; the group became known collectively as the "French ambassadors" and acquired residences in Isfahan and Baghdad, the latter then still under

3. Ibid., 243.
4. Urban VIII, apostolic letter, March 9, 1624: see *A Chronicle of the Carmelites in Persia*, vol. 1, 272–75.

Persian occupation.[5] In correspondence sent from the Persian capital, the Carmelites wrote that "the Augustinians are seen as ambassadors of the King of Spain, the Carmelites as guests sent by the pope, and the Capuchins as envoys of the King of France."[6] The presence of the Latin Church in the Mesopotamian region, and in Persia, was thus secured by the major religious orders: the Carmelites, the Capuchins, and the Augustinians; meanwhile the Dominicans were active in Armenia, and the Jesuits would go to Syria.

The Carmelites made good progress for the Catholic faith in Persia during the reign of Shah Abbas, who took a sincere liking to the Spaniard Juan Taddeo, who had spent twenty-two years in the country, learned to speak the language, and respected the local customs. Wanting a Latin bishop in his kingdom, the king decided to send the same religious back as his own delegate to Rome, requesting the creation of an episcopal see in the Persian capital. On November 2, 1628, Fr. Juan Taddeo left Persia for Rome, carrying with him the shah's letter to Pope Urban VIII. On October 29, 1629, he was received by the pope at Castel Gandolfo, unaware that, in the meantime, Shah Abbas had died.[7] The creation of the first Persian diocese was effected by decree of Propaganda Fide, in recognition of the presence of the various missionaries in the country and the broader pastoral needs of such a wide territory.[8] Juan Taddeo himself seemed ideal for the new role, owing to his unique experience of the land and his knowledge of the language and customs of the people. He was reluctant to accept, believing that a secular priest would

5. *A Chronicle of the Carmelites in Persia*, vol. 1, 283.

6. Ibid., 284.

7. Before dying, Abbas enacted a law whereby any member of a Christian family converting to Islam would immediately inherit the property of the entire family, to the seventh degree. It is estimated that, within twenty years, more than fifty thousand Christians would convert to escape poverty. See Ibid., 288.

8. Approved by Urban VIII on October 2, 1629.

be more suitable, both for representing the Holy See at court, and for preserving harmony among the various religious orders working in the country.

2. The Founding of the Latin Dioceses of Isfahan and of Baghdad (or Babylon); the Latin Bishops of the Persian Era (17th and 18th Centuries)

At the time of his appointment, Juan Taddeo was already fifty-nine years old and in questionable health; so, on the same day of the appointment, he was given a coadjutor, another Carmelite, Timoteo Pérez Vargas, born in Palermo but of Spanish nationality, who was given the title of *episcopus Bagdadi sive Babylonis*.[9] Bernadino Cardinal Spada consecrated the two Carmelites on September 18, 1632, in the Church of the Holy Spirit, at Rome, as the bishops of Isfahan and Baghdad respectively. The borders of the two ecclesiastical territories were established by decree on November 3, 1632, by Propaganda Fide: the bishop of Isfahan would have governance throughout the Persian Empire, but not in Assyria, Armenia, or Georgia; the bishop of Baghdad had jurisdiction over the whole of Assyria and Mesopotamia, from Mosul to Basra, but no competence in Persia, except that conceded to him in writing by the bishop of Isfahan.[10] In the bull of appointment, the pope entrusted Juan Tadeo, now bishop,

9. Michel Le Quien, *Oriens christianus, in quattuor patriarchatus digestus; ecclesiae patriarchae, caeterique praesules totius orientis*, vol. 3 (Paris: Typographia Regia, 1740), coll. 1390–1394. See inter alia, Congregatio Propaganda Fide, *Guide des missions catholiques*, vol. 2 (Paris: l'Œuvre Pontificale de la Propagation de la Foi, 1936), 5. For the remainder of this work, the episcopal titles of "Baghdad" and "Babylon" will be used interchangeably, reflecting the practice of Rome, which used both terms for the same see.

10. Congregatio Progaganda Fide, *Guide des missions catholiques*, vol. 2, 5; and *Chronicle of the Carmelites in Persia*, vol. 1, 301. The borders were subsequently revised by successive decrees on April 29, 1754, and November 16, 1783.

with the task of fostering reconciliation with the various schismatics, heretics, and apostates of his new territory, along with his various other pastoral duties; and, with a letter dated January 9, 1633, the pope commended the new bishops to Shah Safi, who was himself still new in his role. Shah Safi (1629–42) was nineteen years old when he ascended to the throne, and he had a certain respect for the Christian community, and especially the Carmelite missionaries, going as far as writing to the pope praising their work.

These were difficult times, set against the backdrop of the Turkish-Persian War (1630), which created many problems for the religious community of Isfahan and Hamadan. Baghdad itself was threatened, and the Capuchins, who had been trying to establish themselves there since 1629, were in serious danger. In 1638 Baghdad, which had been surrounded by Sultan Murad IV, was conquered by the Turks on December 25. Missionary work in the heart of Mesopotamia was halted by new strict controls on the movements of foreigners. Between spring and summer of 1633, Bishop Juan Taddeo left Rome for Spain, which he intended to visit before returning to Persia, but he died at Lerida on September 5, 1633, without having taken possession of his episcopal see. Upon his death, Timoteo Pérez, as his coadjutor, became bishop of Isfahan. Upon hearing the news, Propaganda Fide began the process of appointing a successor for Pérez in the diocese of Bagdad; and, to avoid the dangers of long journeys through disputed territory, the pope appointed the Carmelite Dimas della Croce, who was already in Persia, as the new bishop of Baghdad. Pérez was thirty-nine years old at the time and, according to his instructions, was to proceed at once to take possession of his new see in Isfahan, but, intimidated by his ignorance of oriental languages, he began to reconsider. While staying in Spain in 1634, he asked Rome for leave to remain in Segovia; and he was eventually relieved of his office by papal decree.[11] If the appointment of Pérez proved improvident, Fr. Dimas della Croce proved to be an even bigger disappointment. He had no episcopal ambitions whatsoever, and he eventually declined the appointment outright, dying shortly thereafter on December 23, 1639, in the convent of Isfahan.

At this time (1585–1642) French policy was under the control of Cardinal Richelieu (1585–1642), who had ambitions for the French crown in the Middle East. The cardinal was determined to counter Portuguese and Dutch influence in the Persian Gulf, and, when the opportunity presented itself, he seized the chance to intervene in Persia and Mesopotamia. In 1629, a wealthy Frenchman named Antoine de Ricouart, a councilor in the Parisian city parliament, died childless and left all his property to his widowed wife Madame Ricouart (née Le Peultre). Madame de Ricouart was a benefactor of the Carmelites of Meaux, whose missionary spirit she especially admired; in 1637, she donated goods equal to six thousand doublons for the foundation of a bishopric among the infidels, on the condition that she be allowed the privilege of selecting the first bishop and that all successors were of French nationality. Pope Urban, sensitive about maintaining good relations with the French and needing to find new sources of funding for the missions, accepted the conditions and the donation with the bull *Super universas* on June 4, 1638, and allocated the funds to provide an annuity for the newly erected diocese of Baghdad (or Babylon).[12] In accord with the first condition of the donation, the pope appointed a Carmelite priest named Bernard de Saint Thérèse (born Jean Duval),[13]

11. He was granted the titular see of Listra, and died at Toledo on April 5, 1651 (see *Chronicle of the Carmelites in Persia*, vol. 1, 340–341).

12. "Ius nominandi ad dictam Ecclesiam personam idoneam quae tamen in Gallia, et non alibi nata semper esse debeat." See Sacrae Congregationis de Propaganda Fide, *Appendix Ad Bullarium Pontificium*, vol. 1 (Rome: Typis Collegii Urbani, n.d.), 216–7; *Chronicle of the Carmelites in Persia*, vol. 1, 342.

13. See Le Quien, *Oriens christianus*, vol. 3, c. 1391. Bishop Bernard was born at Cleméncy, France, on April 22, 1597; he entered the Carmelite com-

as the first bishop of Baghdad, following his nomination by the widow de Ricouart on July 28, 1638.[14] The new bishop received his instructions from Cardinal Richelieu in Paris, in November 1638, along with letters for the Turkish sultan, but he did not leave for Mesopotamia right away; instead he went first to Isfahan, which he hoped to acquire in his own right, now that Pérez had been released from the office.[15]

The journey from Constantinople to Isfahan took him through Armenia, where he met the local catholicos, Philip, to whom he delivered a letter from Urban VIII (April 19, 1640) on the question of union with Rome. Philip received him graciously, but was cool on the idea of union. When he arrived in the Persian capital in July 1640, the new bishop was received by Shah Safi, to whom he took an immediate liking for his gentle manner, humanistic cultural impulses, and his learned knowledge of the sciences. Initially the prelate chose to live with the Carmelites, but after a few months he made different arrangements; and, October 9, 1641, he took possession of a property,

---

munity at Rue de Vaugirad, Paris, in 1611, and became both a scholar and a preacher; he won the favor of both Cardinal Richelieu and Queen Anne of Austria, and was Madame de Ricouart's confessor when she proposed him as the first bishop of the new diocese. For a fuller biography, see *Chronicle of the Carmelites in Persia*, vol. 2, 818–24.

14. He was consecrated bishop by Cardinal Pallotta on August 22 of that year, in the Church of St. Sylvester at Rome. One month later, on September 25, 1638, the pope named him Apostolic Vicar of Isfahan as well, and gave him the faculty to live in Isfahan instead of Baghdad (see *Chronicle of the Carmelites in Persia*, vol. 1, 342–43). Mesopotamia and Persia were ecclesiastically untied from 1638 until 1693, and again from 1789 until 1874. See P. Lesourd, *Histoire des missions catholiques* (Paris: Librairie de l'Arc, 1937), 203.

15. He left Paris for Marseille on July 10, 1639, sailing for Malta, Smyrna, and Constantinople, arriving on September 2 of the following year; there he began to have misgivings about the difficulty of governing both Isfahan and Baghdad, since the first was under Persian rule and the other under Turkish control. When Baghdad became part of the Ottoman Empire on December 26, 1638, this ended up being a permanent state of affairs, and that city became the seat of a powerful governorship.

purchased in the name of the king of France, which became part episcopal residence and part church. When opening the building, Bernard made clear the French connection of his new ministry by publicly displaying Richelieu's personal insignia and appointing him "the first cathedral protector."[16] The new cathedral church was dedicated to the Blessed Virgin Mary and consecrated on December 8, 1641, in the presence of the Dominican archbishop of Noxivan, as well as the local Augustinians, Capuchins, and Carmelites. While the day itself was marked as a great feast for the Catholics of Isfahan, the moment soon passed. In the spring of 1942, having been in the diocese only a few months, Bernard decided to return to France.[17] On the way back, he took the road to Hamadan and reached Baghdad, where he had the satisfaction of celebrating Mass for some of the members of his flock. He reached Aleppo in June of 1642. While his departure was a great disappointment, Bernard intended to return; he hoped that by returning to France he could obtain financial aid for the foundation of a missionary seminary in Persia and bring some religious brothers back with him. This plan collapsed when he discovered, upon his arrival in Paris, that his patron Cardinal Richelieu had died and there was no one willing to support his plan. He remained in France until 1645, while Rome continued to urge him to return to his diocese. Once again the selection of bishops for Persia and Mesopotamia had not been successful.

It would be a century before a bishop of Baghdad took up permanent residence in his see. While the diocese was created

16. See *Chronicle of the Carmelites in Persia*, vol. 1, 347.
17. He left citing the medical concerns, including kidney stones; the personal animosity of the Dutch representative, whom he accused of trying to poison him; and an attack with a scimitar, which left him with lingering wounds. He also cited the behavior of the local Christians, whose morality he felt left much to be desired. After delivering the house and the church to care of the Augustinian prior, who had returned to Isfahan, he departed.

with the best of ecclesiastical intentions, the conditions could not really have been any worse: the political and military situation in Mesopotamia was very unstable and in the throes of hard and bloody conflicts; persecution and intolerance placed real limitations on the Church and came from both civil authorities and schismatic Christians, neither of whom took kindly to the establishment of a Catholic presence in the region. However, from the missionary point of view, the Church continued to grow: the Carmelites increased their work among then Armenian and Nestorian Christians, as well as the Mandaeans, while the Capuchins had been at work at Mosul since 1639, with two brothers living in the city. These religious had no churches, or any formal place of worship, since the Turks forbade their construction or reconstruction; their pastoral activity took place entirely underground, in the greatest secrecy. In Mosul, at that time, there were some five hundred Christian families, of which about three hundred were Nestorians and two hundred Jacobites. Nevertheless, they appreciated the presence of the friars, though they were regarded with suspicion by the local pasha, who, from time to time, would concoct allegations against them and throw them into prison. The Capuchins had a similar experience in Baghdad, where they were imprisoned by the governor in 1658.[18]

Meanwhile, back in France, Bishop Bernard, now suffering from various infirmities, was given permission to remain in Europe and invited to either resign or to choose a coadjutor. While he initially suggested the prior of the Augustinians in Isfahan, he found no one willing to accept the appointment; in the end the choice fell on the Carmelite Michel du Saint Esprit, who, upon his appointment on June 2, 1650, resigned almost immediately.[19] It was not until May 30, 1661, that Rome was able

18. *Chronicle of the Carmelites in Persia*, vol. 1, 392.
19. Sacrae Congregatio de Propaganda Fide, *Annales de l'Association de la Propagation de la Foi*, vol. 2 (1826), 3.

to find a candidate for the see of Baghdad in the Benedictine Dom Placide-Louis du Chemin. Bishop Bernard died on April 11, 1669, renowned for his piety and for his missionary zeal.[20]

At the time of his appointment as coadjutor bishop with right of succession in Baghdad (May 30, 1661), and as apostolic administrator of Isfahan, where he would reside, the Benedictine Dom Placid Louis du Chemin (1669–83) was sixty-five years old and a professor of theology. Pope Alexander VII gave him the titular see of Neocaesarea *in partibus infidelium* and informed Shah Abbas II of the choice in an apostolic letter dated July 16, 1661.[21] The hope that this would end the constant confusion in the episcopal sees of Mesopotamia was short lived; indeed, the situation soon became worse than before. The new bishop immediately began to put off his departure, claiming—despite the aid he had received—a lack of funds; he then returned to Paris and, citing legal reasons, would not leave.[22] Five years later (1667), he was still in France. In June of 1670, he started calling himself "Patriarch of Babylon," though his claim to the title was refused by Rome. Meanwhile, the diocese of Isfahan had now languished without a bishop for twenty-seven years. Though it

20. Despite his health, Bernard continued with his plan to form missionaries, believing that religious communities were not producing enough members dedicated to the work. As part of his plan, he used the personal wealth of religious for the creation of a seminary, which was incorporated into the Institute of Foreign Missions in Paris, located on the road that, even today, in honor of his episcopal title, is named Rue de Babylone (ibid., 9, 53–54).

21. *Chronicle of the Carmelites in Persia*, vol. 1, 402; Le Quien, *Oriens christianus*, vol. 3, col. 1392.

22. *Annales de l'Archevêché de Bagdad rédigées par mgr. Lion, A. de B.* (Administrateur de Babylone), manuscript, 1–50, in NA deposit Iraq in ASV, 3–5. In 2012 all the archives of the apostolic nunciature to Iraq were transferred to the Vatican Secret Archives, where they constitute a deposit in cataloging. In references these will be cited as NA deposit Iraq in ASV, *Annales de l'Archevêché*, and *Histoire de l'Archevêché*. (The author quotes archival documents in various languages, usually Latin or Italian. The translations into English are the work of the translator—Trans.)

was still hoped that du Chemin might agree to serve, on June 26, 1674, Propaganda Fide decided to appoint an apostolic vicar for Baghdad and Isfahan with episcopal dignity. This title was given to François Piquet. Meanwhile, the congregation canonically proceeded against du Chemin, depriving him of his office. In the end, du Chemin died at Paris in 1683 and is remembered as a terrible example of episcopal conduct.

To François Piquet (1684–1685), consecrated bishop on September 26, 1677, the apostolic see entrusted the pastoral care of Baghdad as well as other tasks proper to an apostolic visitor to the region.[23] He also represented the French king, Louis XIV, in the court of the shah of Persia, where he interceded for Christians in the face of Islamic authorities seeking to compel them into apostasy through taxation and other economic sanctions. This situation was so bad that Innocent XI made a personal plea for the cause of the Christians under Persian rule. Leaving Marseille, Bishop Piquet passed through Alexandretta, Aleppo, and Diarbekir, before finally arriving at Tabriz. His new brief included managing the ongoing disputes between the Syriac-Catholic patriarchate and the Orthodox, dealing with the Armenian province of Noxivan,[24] and handling the case of

23. Born at Lyon on April 17, 1626, at the time of his appointment he was serving as secretary of the seminary of the Foreign Missions. Piquet was a man known for wisdom and zeal; he knew the Middle East well, having served as French consul at Aleppo (1652–60), and even as a layman had performed many services for the Catholic Church. While in Rome on consular business, he was received with honor by the pope, who described the problems and the condition of Christians. Piquet immediately renounced his consular role and embraced the ecclesiastical state, receiving holy orders at the age of forty. He was elected bishop by Pope Clement X on December 22, 1674, and was given the titular see of Cesaropoli *in partibus* and made administrator of the Latin diocese of Baghdad by papal bull on July 31, 1675.

24. Concerning the Noxivan Christians, Piquet wrote on October 8, 1681: "The poor treatment, extortion, and tyranny of these Persian rulers is continuous, and perhaps even harder than that of the Turks, at least with respect to the religious and the poor Catholic population; for this reason they

the metropolitan of Amid, Yousuf, who, thanks to the missionary activity of the Capuchins, had embraced the Catholic faith along with much of his clergy and faithful. Yousuf's cause was pleaded to Propaganda Fide, who secured him "the title of the Chaldean Patriarch, as agreed with the Syrian patriarch."[25] Thus the bishop became a patriarch with the title of Yusuf I (1681–96); first of what was to become the Yousuf line.

In October of 1681, Piquet took part in the election of the new archbishop of Noxivan, a Dominican named Sebastian Knab; and it was not until July of 1682 that he arrived at Isfahan, seven years after being appointed coadjutor. In a letter dated March 25, 1683, the bishop described to Innocent XI the welcome they received and the audience granted to him by the shah, "who sent greetings to the King of France (Louis XIV)."[26] In Isfahan, Piquet then received news of his appointment as bishop of Baghdad (1684), which became possible after the death of du Chemin. He took his oath of office before the superior of the Jesuits of Isfahan, informing Rome that it would be difficult to go "above all into Baghdad, which is always full of soldiers"[27] and that attempting to enter the city would be further complicated by his diplomatic mission to the shah of Persia, sworn enemy of the Turks who then occupied Baghdad.

However, he made it clear that he was willing to obey if the pope commanded him to go to his new see. He was well aware of the conditions faced by the Christians in Hamadan and

---

pressure me greatly to speak to the king in their defense" (*Chronicle of the Carmelites in Persia*, vol. 1, 417).

25. *Annales de l'Archevêché*, 12 e 56; Le Quien, *Oriens christianus*, vol. 2, coll. 1161–1162: "an. 1681 ab Innocentio Papa XI, die 20 Maii Chaldaeorum Patriarcha constitutus, pallioque donatus ..." Evidently, when Piquet was writing at Rome on June 3, 1681, he was not yet aware that Innocent XI had already recognized the archbishop as patriarch on May 20.

26. *Chronicle of the Carmelites in Persia*, vol. 1, 430; also *Annales de l'Archevêché*, 13 and 56.

27. *Annales de l'Archevêché*, 14 and 56.

that the Armenian community was in urgent need of spiritual help. Piquet made it his special preoccupation to consider how to get to Baghdad to take up residence there. He did eventually get to Hamadan on January 7, 1685, but died unexpectedly a few months later. Once again, the diocese of Baghdad became vacant just two and a half years after being filled. Before dying, Piquet had requested a coadjutor in the person of Father Pidou, a former coworker,[28] whose name was included among a list of potential episcopal candidates, and whom Innocent XI eventually made a bishop. Louis-Marie Pidou de Saint Olon, CR,[29] a respected religious, spoke Arabic, Turkish, and Armenian, having been a missionary for thirty years, especially among the Armenians of Poland, and had been rector of the Armenian College in Lviv for ten years. Of noble family, his brother, Monsieur de Saint Olon, was an officer of the court under Louis XIV. Pidou was in Constantinople when he was invited by Piquet to join him in Hamadan, where he arrived in January 1685. In a report on the situation to Pope Innocent XI, Propaganda Fide proposed to the pope that he appoint Pidou as Latin bishop of Baghdad, praising his zeal, as well as his knowledge of local customs and language. The proposal was accepted on November 24, 1687.

The move was strongly resisted by Pidou, who asked the papal nuncio in Paris to persuade Rome against his appointment, believing that a Carmelite would be more effective in that diocese. Yet, out of obedience to Rome, he remained in Hamadan from 1687 to 1689, when he went to Isfahan to receive episcopal consecration from the archbishop of Noxivan, the Dominican Paul Baptiste Avanian. As a new bishop, simultaneously bishop of Baghdad and apostolic administrator of Isfahan, he soon found himself struggling with the management of the two dio-

28. *Chronicle of the Carmelites in Persia*, vol. 1, 433.
29. Born at Paris in 1637, Pidou was fifty years old when he was appointed bishop of Baghdad on November 24, 1687; he died in 1717.

ceses and their churches. Pope Innocent XI offered a pastoral solution in October 1693, by appointing the Carmelite friar Elia de St. Albert as bishop of Isfahan.

A permanent episcopal presence in Isfahan had become a necessity for the defense of the Catholic community, who were under pressure both from the schismatic Armenians and the religiously intolerant Governor Husain. Meanwhile, in Baghdad, the presence of the ordinary was urgently needed, not only because the seat had been vacant for so long but because of the harsh Turkish religious policy toward the Christians of Mesopotamia. Pidou wrote to the pope via his brother, pointing out that, with the Turks in Baghdad and Basra in the hands of the Arabs, perhaps the latter city would serve as an alternative venue for the see of Baghdad; but the idea was not approved. In July 1706 Pidou returned to Hamadan; and, because of his age and infirmity, Rome decided to appoint a coadjutor, proposing a priest from Angers, a professor at the Sorbonne, who was about forty years old. The proposal was accepted and approved by Clement XI, who, on June 27, 1707, appointed Gratien de Gallisson as coadjutor of Baghdad; he received episcopal consecration on October 8, 1708. He left for the East and, on his arrival in Isfahan, he obtained from the shah a decree recognizing the rights of the missions as coming under the protection of the king of France, ending the more formal forms of persecution.[30] His diplomatic triumph was a great relief for the missions and

30. *Chronicle of the Carmelites in Persia*, vol. 1, 537. The recognition of the protection of the rights of Christians in the Ottoman Empire was part of the so-called Concessions which came about as part of a series of treaties concluded with European powers. Since 1500, France, beginning with Louis XII, had been working—first with the Mamluk Sultanate of Cairo, and then with the Ottoman Empire—to secure recognition of the rights of Christians under the Sublime Porte. Under Louis XIV the French missionaries multiplied their presence and activities in the Ottoman territories, and, in 1673, French subjects were protected in their functions and no one was permitted to cause them harm. For this reason, the French bishops of Mesopotamia or Persia often sought some consular office from the king of France.

gave the wider Christian community, religious and lay, high hopes for the future of the Church in Persia. Sadly, de Gallisson died unexpectedly on September 22, 1712.

Two years after the death of de Gallisson, Rome decided to provide the elderly Pidou with a new coadjutor, and selected the Capuchin Timothée de la Fléche. He was appointed by a papal bull signed by Pope Clement XI on May 29, 1715, making him coadjutor of Baghdad, but once he was ordained, the new bishop asked Joseph-Emmanuel Cardinal de la Trémoille to intercede on his behalf, saying he wished to enter monastic life and that his age would not stand up to such a long journey. He resigned shortly thereafter. Of the two coadjutors given to Pidou, the first had died prematurely and the second had resigned before he even left. Given the shambles the situation had become, on April 26, 1718, Rome decided to appoint a new successor for Pidou, a zealous and pious pastor, and a religious with a heart full of missionary spirit.

The name of Dominique-Marie Varlet had already been discussed in Rome as a possible coadjutor bishop for Pidou. According to the information available in Rome, he was known as a good and pious priest, about forty years old, educated and practiced in oriental languages. He had experience as an apostolic missionary in America and was vicar general of the bishop of Quebec. Pope Clement XI accepted the proposal, and on August 29, 1718, he gave his assent, appointing him titular bishop of Ascalon and coadjutor with right of succession in Baghdad, though the news of the death of Pidou would not reach Rome until 1719. When he heard the news of his election, Varlet was quite astonished, but, in a letter dated January 29, 1719, he promised that he would go to his diocese as soon as possible. Unfortunately, Rome had been grossly misinformed about Varlet, who was an incorrigible Jansenist. Rome sought to remedy the situation through the nuncio in Paris, requiring Varlet to report there to receive his papal instructions and swear an oath of allegiance to *Unigenitus*,[31] but instead he went straight to Holland, where he immediately ordained several Jansenist priests and administered the sacrament of confirmation in their oratory. Propaganda Fide, seriously alarmed, instructed the bishop of Isfahan, Barnabas de Fidelis, to immediately suspend and interdict Varlet upon his arrival. Hearing of the reception waiting for him as he passed through Qazwin, Varlet decided to go back to Holland,[32] where he died a schismatic and contumacious in his disobedience to the Apostolic See. Thus, the third candidate to succeed Pidou proved an even greater disappointment than the previous two, leading Rome, finally, to the understanding that it would be far better to look for suitable candidates among the missionaries already working in the Levant, rather than to seek them anywhere else.

3. The Bishops of the Mesopotamian Period (18th–19th Centuries); the Carmelite, Capuchin, and Dominican Missionaries

The death of Pidou ended the series of resident bishops in Persia, and it would be another quarter of a century before a new bishop was consecrated for Baghdad. During the episcopate of Pidou, the Baghdad Capuchins had been forced to abandon the city for the third time; and the faithful poor of the city were left without religious assistance. Because of the difficulties of providing a bishop for Baghdad, Innocent XIII appointed an apostolic vicar and entrusted the task to the Discalced Carmelite Joseph-Marie de Jésus (1721). The priest had been provincial of the Carmelite

31. Clement XI's bull condemning the 101 Jansenist propositions of Quesnel's thesis. *Chronicle of the Carmelites in Persia*, vol. 1, 550.

32. In 1722 the nuncio in Brussels reported him as being in the company of Pesquier Quesnel, a known Jansenist, with whom he "always professed the same sentiments" (*Annales de l'Archevêché*, 29; *Chronicle of the Carmelites in Persia*, vol. 1, 550–51).

mission in Persia (1709–13), and the news reached him while he was on his way to found a new mission in Lebanon and Syria. Retracing his steps from Aleppo, he reached Diarbekir and then headed to Mosul, staying for a few days,[33] and finally reaching Baghdad on May 20, 1722, where he stayed for four months.[34] There he found that the faithful had been left to themselves for fifteen years, following the persecution of the Capuchins.[35] After a four-month stay, Father Joseph-Marie went to Basra to ensure that the Carmelite mission was in good condition, he was satisfied with what he found, although liturgically the Christians of that city follow the Julian instead of the Gregorian calendar.[36] But he soon found himself locked in Basra; he could

33. He spent twenty days hearing confessions and teaching the catechism. The Catholics of Mosul had also been without religious assistance since the death of the last Capuchin in the city nine years earlier. The Christians of Mosul were mostly Nestorans and Jacobites, who had five old churches (*Chronicle of the Carmelites in Persia*, vol. 1, 552).

34. This was during the governorship of Hasan Pasha. Not having permission to reside in the city, the apostolic vicar had to face many difficulties and celebrate Mass in secret. According to him, they were "very devout to the Church of Rome" and rarely professed "heretical doctrines." Some of the faithful, who had gone to the "heretical Churches" out of necessity, posed the question whether, in the absence of Catholic priests, the faithful could receive communion from the Nestorians, "knowing that the Nestorian priests do not have valid consecration (as among the Latins) because they only say that the Holy Spirit will descend upon the sacred species" (*Annales de l'Archevêché*, 34; *Histoire de l'Archevêché*, 60–61).

35. In Baghdad there were two sacred buildings, one Nestorian, the other Armenian. According to the apostolic vicar, the Nestorian community was divided into two, and, of the two, the majority of the people were Catholic, but the priests were appointed by the heretical patriarch (see *Chronicle of the Carmelites in Persia*, vol. 2, 1252), although "one of these priests who says he is Catholic asked if he can give communion to the heretics who call themselves Catholic. The Nestorian priests say they are Catholic in heart and feeling and their only error is in praying for the Nestorian priest (patriarch) Eliya, who has allowed Catholics to attend his churches, and not making mention of (the patriarch) Catholic Yousuf" (*Annales de l'Archevêché*, 35).

36. The Gregorian calendar was introduced by Pope Gregory XIII in 1582 with the bull *Inter gravissimas*, which replaced the Julian calendar.

not proceed to Hamadan because of tensions between Persians and Turks, nor return to Baghdad, because the roads were controlled by the Arabs. Persia itself was in a state of confusion.[37] In a letter dated November 1723, the apostolic vicar reported that Christians had fled Hamadan, and he lacked news from all the missions, including Isfahan. In November of the following year, he wrote that Hamadan was taken by the Turks and destroyed and that Father Jean-Joseph de Jésus, who had care of the house built by Bishop Pidou, had been taken captive when the house was ransacked.[38] These tensions would continue for years to come, though the Christian community remained faithful, fueled by the admirable life of these missionaries.

Returning to Baghdad after a trip to Aleppo (1727), Father Joseph-Marie de Jésus wrote to Rome asking to be replaced, recalling that he had accepted his office reluctantly and only because Giuseppe Cardinal Sacripante, of Propaganda Fide, had assured him that it would only be temporary. In his letter, he also noted that he did not have either physical or mental strength to continue in the role, which was itself made more difficult because the title of apostolic vicar was unknown in those lands, and he could not command the necessary respect or authority. He proposed, in his stead, the appointment of Fr. Urbano, superior of the Carmelites of Persia, as bishop, despite the fact that Varlet, though a schismatic and now excommunicated, had not yet formally given up the title.

In August 1728, Benedict XIII, having accepted the resignation of the apostolic vicar, designated as successor Bernard-Marie de Jésus, bishop of Oea (modern Tripoli), authorizing a Dis-

37. So says the apostolic vicar in a letter dated July 1, 1723, from Basra (see *Chronicle of the Carmelites in Persia*, vol. 1, 583).
38. The house was later returned, but the religious had to take on a great amount of debt to redeem it (see *Chronicle of the Carmelites in Persia*, vol. 1, 583).

calced Carmelite to serve as pro-vicar for him. The general of the order proposed Fr. Emmanuel a S. Alberto (née Baillet, a.k.a Balliet or Ballyet) of Burgundy. Though young, Emmanuel was learned and considered well-prepared for the role. A papal bull was issued on July 31, 1728, appointing Bishop Bernard-Marie de Jésus as apostolic vicar of Baghdad, without a residence requirement (due to age), to be represented by a "pro-apostolic vicar" in the person of the Carmelite Emmanuel Saint Albert. Emmanuel, in light of the difficult conditions in which the missionaries were forced to live in Baghdad, decided to ask for the protection of the French authorities and obtained from the viceroy of the Indies (stationed at Pondicherry) protective letters and gifts for the pasha of Baghdad.[39] He was well received in Baghdad, and the Turkish governor allowed him to buy a home in the Christian neighborhood, where he took up residence, annexing a chapel dedicated to the apostle Saint Thomas. On July 14, he laid the foundation stone for the cathedral of Baghdad, the construction of which, with much hard work and sacrifice, lasted twenty years. It would still be Fr. Emmanuel, though as bishop in his own right, who would eventually consecrate it.[40] In October 1731 he wrote to Propaganda Fide: "We have restored the (Capuchin) mission in Baghdad, lost more than twenty years ago." The Christian community at that time was composed of one hundred fifty families, of which about thirty were Catholic and the remainder were Armenian, Nestorian, and Jacobite.[41]

39. *Chronicle of the Carmelites in Persia*, vol. 2, 1252–1253. "In order to found this mission (in Baghdad) on a stable and advantageous basis … you considered that the only method would be to address a petition to the viceroy of France of the East Indies, in order to obtain a letter of recommendation to the governor of Baghdad, to grant us every freedom" (ibid., vol. 1, 619).

40. *Chronicle of the Carmelites in Persia*, vol. 1, 619. The house purchased in the Christian quarter was in ruins, but still cost 500 gold crowns (ibid., vol. 2, 1253; *Annales de l'Archevêché*, 43).

41. *Chronicle of the Carmelites in Persia*, vol. 2, 1252; *Histoire de l'Archevêché*, 63.

This community suffered greatly in the following years (1732–36) during the wars between the Turks and Persians: twice the Persian general Quli Khan laid siege to Baghdad, while the Turks led numerous raids into Persia and against the small Catholic missions of that land. It is here that the Carmelite Jean-Joseph, a missionary for fifteen years in Hamadan, was said to have died of starvation. The Turkish-Persian war—which in the meantime had grown to encompass Basra—ended unpredictably in 1735, when a British gunboat, at anchor in the Shatt al-Arab, intervened against the Persians on the orders of the British consul, forcing the Persians to beat their retreat. In gratitude, the consul was invited to Baghdad by the Turkish governor, where he took advantage of his newfound prestige to give considerable support to the Catholic mission.[42] In Baghdad, Fr. Emmanuel set himself to forge good relations with the local authorities; this was helped by him becoming the French consul, a legal status that helped elevate him above harassment and religious jealousies.[43] He was known to be a generous pastor, especially during the cholera epidemic that afflicted the city, and in which he was himself infected.

Meanwhile, the Jansenist Bishop Varlet finally died in 1742, leaving the see of Baghdad formally vacant, and allowing Benedict XIV to appoint Fr. Emmanuel de Saint Albert as bishop (1742–73). The episcopal dignity and diplomatic status he enjoyed enabled him to intervene on behalf of the Christian community on numerous occasions, and he brought many Syrians, Nestorians, and Armenians back to the Catholic faith. He was a wise shepherd, enterprising and zealous; his only complaint

42. *Chronicle of the Carmelites in Persia*, vol. 1, 604; vol 2, 1195; *Annales de l'Archevêché*, 46–47.
43. In a 1740 treaty with France, the Turkish Sultan Mahmud I declared that the French bishops and religious living in the Ottoman Empire would be protected and no one could stop them from practicing their faith in their own churches and or in other places where they lived.

was for more missionary personnel and for Rome to launch a permanent mission in Mosul, urging that the Capuchins return to the work that they had been forced to abandon twenty years earlier.[44] In August of 1747, Rome sent three Carmelites with instructions to resume relations with the Chaldean Patriarch Yousuf III (Timothy Maroge, a resident of Amid) and asked for two Chaldean students to be sent for studies in the Urban College in Rome, one from Mardin and the other from Mosul. The Dominican Order was also equally interested in opening missions in Mosul and Kurdistan, where they immediately sent some Italian friars, who worked nearly a century (1748–1857).

During his thirty years of pastoral life, Emmanuel served the community of Mesopotamia (Iraq) tirelessly; and when Baghdad was afflicted by the plague in 1772, the bishop became a victim. Providence had decided to crown his life with the most glorious sacrifice to which a pastor can aspire: to sacrifice his life for his sheep. The septuagenarian bishop died on April 4, 1773, while caring for the sick, "a martyr of duty and charity."[45] According to his fellow Carmelites, he was one of the most active missionaries that the order ever had in the Near Levant missions of the seventeenth and eighteenth centuries. He was a man of great ability and his memory lived long in the Christian community. He was also much esteemed by the Ottoman authorities, who granted him residence and freedom of worship.[46]

It is from the time of Emmanuel's ministry as bishop that the Latin Church of Mesopotamia dates the foundation of the Dominican mission in Mosul. A Chaldean priest had asked Benedict XIV to send Dominican fathers for his territory, and,

44. *Chronicle of the Carmelites in Persia*, vol. 1, 623.

45. *Chronicle of the Carmelites in Persia*, vol. 2, 1260; *Histoire de l'Archevêché*, 66. According to the Dominican Leopoldo Soldini (April 16, 1773), many thousands of people died during the plague epidemic in Baghdad and Mosul (*Chronicle of the Carmelites in Persia*, vol. 2, 1260).

46. *Chronicle of the Carmelites in Persia*, vol. 2, 1253.

in response, the general of the Order of Preachers sent the Italians Francesco Turriani and Domenico Codeleoncini in 1748. They were joined by Fathers Giuseppe Campanile and Domenico Lanza,[47] the latter as an apostolic prefect, in which capacity he was credentialed by the Turkish authorities in 1756. Lanza's presence inaugurated an era of great development for the Dominican missions and for the Catholic community. If the first few years were made very hard for these missionaries by the epidemics that plagued the region, they were rewarded by the number of conversions which they made among the many villages in the Plain of Nineveh (Batnaia, Telkief, Tellskof, Alqosh, Bacofa) and in the mountains of Kurdistan (Amadia, Zakho). It was the zeal of the Dominicans during these years which spurred the conversion even of some Nestorian and Syrian Orthodox bishops, who brought their communities with them into Catholicism, strengthening the number of Churches in the region which were in communion with the pope.[48] In 1760, the Dominican Leopoldo Soldini founded a mission for Kurdistan in Amadia, with his colleague Maurizio Garzoni.[49] Garzoni would live there for fourteen years and compose a 4,600-word Italian-Kurdish dictionary and grammar after having confessed it had been "difficult and painful to learn a language without the material help of some grammar, or book, because the Kurds use for their own writings a literal form of Persian, which is not understood among them, except by their teachers."[50] Accord-

47. Domenico Lanza (1718–82) was a historian; Giuseppe Campanile (1762–1835) became the author of a *History of the Kurdistan Region* and the religious sects existing there.

48. According to the testimony of Bishop Emmanuel, on his arrival in Mesopotamia, in 1729, there were 60,000 Catholics. This rose to almost 100,000 by 1753 (schismatics amounted to 300,000); the highest concentration of Catholics was in Mosul, where the Dominicans had not yet established a church, and in the nearby villages.

49. Leopoldo Soldini was a Venetian doctor, botanist, and mathematician, he died at Zakho in 1779; Maurizio Garzoni lived from 1734 to 1804.

50. Maurizio Garzoni, *Grammatica e vocabolario della lingua kurda*

ing to an account by Garzoni, in Kurdistan there were so many Christians "they number more than a hundred thousand; most of them ... Nestorians divided into two patriarchates. One being the patriarchate of ... Mar S(h)imon with five suffragan bishops; the other ... Mar Eli(y)a ... (with jurisdiction) in four principalities of Kurdistan ... (and) throughout Mesopotamia. (They) even have Jacobites among them, with their respective bishops, and many Armenians."[51] A few years later, in 1779, Garzoni was made apostolic prefect of the mission in Zakho, upon the death of Soldini, whom he revered and loved as a father.[52]

From 1773 to 1820, the Latin Church in Baghdad had no bishop. The closest the see came to being filled was in 1781, when the Benedictine Jean-Baptiste Miroudot du Bourg was consecrated and appointed, but almost immediately deposed and canonically prosecuted for having participated in the illicit consecration of the archbishop of Paris, who had sworn allegiance to the new constitution during the throes of the French Revolution. Miroudot never made it to Baghdad, where the pastoral care of the faithful remained in the care of the Carmelite fathers, some of whom served as apostolic vicars.[53]

On June 10, 1820, Pope Pius VII appointed Fr. Pierre-Alexandre

---

composti dal padre Maurizio Garzoni de' Predicatori ex-missionario apostolico (Roma: Sacra Congregazione di Propaganda Fide, 1787), 7–8. The dictionary is a key work because it represents the first recognition of the originality of the Kurdish language; for this reason, Fr. Garzoni is often called the "father of Kurdology" (see Linguistic and Oriental Studies in Honour of Fabrizio A. Pennacchietti, ed. P. G. Bobone, A. Mengozzi, and M. Tosco [Wiesbaden: Harrassowitz, 2006], 293).

51. Garzoni, Grammatica, 6–7.

52. Fr. Soldini was buried at Zakho, which was then a town of ten thousand inhabitants. His memory was preserved for a long time in that region, both for his brave missionary work and for the charitable work he undertook among poor (see G. Campanile, Storia della regione del Kurdistan [Napoli: Stamperia dei fratelli Fernandes, 1818], 57).

53. One of these, Fr. Fulgenzio di Santa Maria, while serving as apostolic pro-vicar in Baghdad in August 1800, noted that Chaldean church had been completely destroyed by the Turkish authorities, leaving the Carmelite

Coupperie, of the Congregation of the Missionaries of Mary of Blessed Louis de Montfort, as the new Latin bishop of Baghdad. The pope made the choice in response to "serious disorders which have disturbed the Latin Church of Babylon, and which call for the prompt allocation of a new pastor, who will, through the exercise of apostolic zeal, assume the task of leading these people along the road to health, with sound doctrine and by example of Christian virtue."[54] Coupperie was expected to receive episcopal ordination and take up residence in Baghdad as soon as possible and he arrived in 1821. At this time, Baghdad was a city with 150,000 inhabitants; the Christian population was made up mostly of Chaldeans and Nestorians, along with sizable Syrian and Armenian communities. Additionally there was only one Latin church, administered by the Carmelites. In June of 1823, the now Bishop Coupperie was offered the vacant French consulship for the city. While Propaganda Fide actually opposed the appointment, believing that the position was incompatible with canonical norms, Coupperie himself believed that the circumstances in which he was working made a compelling argument for an exception to the rules. Pope Leo XII agreed, granting him a special derogation to assume the office of consul general of France in Baghdad.

---

house as the only Christian place of worship in the city (see *Chronicle of the Carmelites in Persia*, vol. 2, 1260).

54. Quoted from a letter from Propaganda Fide dated June 10, 1820. See also another letter from Propaganda Fide, September 10, 1820. According to a communication from Propaganda Fide on November 24, 1821, this was in response to the case of a Carmelite priest named Sigismund di San Carlo who posed the "danger of serious disorders"; the Carmelite "as apostolic vicar (of Baghdad) ... (had begun) to show disobedience to this Sacred Congregation." Fr. Sigismund had friends in Baghdad, where he practiced medicine among the poor and maintained good relations with the authorities, who defended him; and he continually evaded orders, both from his superior and from Propaganda Fide, to return to Rome. He even sought the protection of the pasha. He finally departed from Baghdad and went to Mosul, where he died, in 1823. See NA deposit Iraq in ASV.

Coupperie's first years as bishop were very hard on him. He was already sixty years old, and the climate, the lack of religious cooperators, the size of the territory, the difficult and dangerous journeys he had to undertake, all strained his endurance. He asked to be allowed to step down, but Leo XII rejected his resignation and encouraged him to continue; he had important work to do resolving the disputes between the different Churches, encouraging respect for the rights of particular rites, and helping address the vacancy of the patriarchate of the Chaldean Church.[55] He was also told to verify the request for ecclesiastical communion presented to Rome by the Nestorian Patriarch Shimon XVII Abraham and a group of Nestorian and Jacobite bishops and monks; a happy prospect, if it could be brought to fruition.[56] The thorniest question concerned the Chaldean patriarchate; the archbishop Hormizd Yohannan, who had converted to Catholicism, aspired to the title of patriarch of Babylon of the Chaldeans.[57] Rome wanted Coupperie to assess his intentions, which he did and found them to be sincere. Pope Pius VIII granted Yohannan the patriarchal title in 1830, allowing a significant part of the Eastern Church to resume full communion with Rome.[58] The same year also saw the beginning of the legal emancipation for the non-Catholic patriarchs and formal recognition of the Chaldeans and Syrians by the Sublime Porte.

55. Letter from Propaganda Fide, April 30, 1825, in NA deposit Iraq in ASV.

56. Letter from Propaganda Fide, July 30, 1825, in NA deposit Iraq in ASV.

57. Letter from Propaganda Fide, May 13, 1826. in NA deposit Iraq in ASV.

58. Letters from Propaganda Fide, May 13, 1826; March 28, 1829; May 5, 1829; all found in NA deposit Iraq in ASV. Pope Leo XII actually approved the conferral of the title but died without publishing it in a consistory; his successor, Pius VIII, confirmed the decision and granted him the sacred pallium, recognizing him as patriarch of Babylon of the Chaldeans on July 5, 1830 (letters from Propaganda Fide, May 15, 1830; August 7, 1830; in NA deposit Iraq in ASV).

In 1844, an agreement established civil and administrative personality for the three communities (Armenian, Chaldean, and Syrian) and their respective patriarchs were granted the right of *bérat*.[59] In 1826, Bishop Coupperie visited Mosul and the monks of the cave-monastery of St. Ormisda, for whom he secured apostolic approval of their rule and constitution. He then visited the Christian villages of Alqosh and Amadia, returning with favorable impressions which he related in long reports on the status and development of the Catholic missions.[60] In response to the pastoral demands of the diocese, which had an acute shortage of priests, Coupperie asked for help from the Chaldean monks,[61] while at the same time putting his full support behind restoring the education program initiated by the Carmelites. He was also quick to recognize the value of religious women's congregations for pastoral ministry. Additionally, he founded the Servants of God, to whom he gave a rule of life full of wisdom and piety. He believed that the mission in Mesopotamia did not require courage so much as patience, and he identified five priorities: development of vocations, support for bishops and priests in their spiritual and material needs, redemption of Christians sold into Muslim slavery for debt, pastoral care of Christians in remote

59. *Bérat* is diplomatic recognition by the Sublime Porte, conferring dignity, authority, and privileges enjoyed by other non-Catholic communities. The Catholic bishops were granted the right to participate in the District Administrative Council, and the Christians of the three communities were given access to the administrative and municipal consuls, as well as to the courts of first instance and of commerce (see V. Cuinet, *La Turquie d'Asie—Géographie Administrative*, vol. 2 [Paris: Ernest Leroux, 1891], 771).

60. See *Annales de l'Association de la Propagation de la Foi*, 1823–34.

61. According to the Chaldean priest Paul Elia Makdassi of Nineveh (Mosul), St. Ormisda monastery was home to eighty monks. They were well known for their piety, zeal, culture, and knowledge of languages, all of which they put at the disposal of the evangelization in the Kurdish regions, stretching from Persia up to Kabul and India, bringing Manichaeans, Yazidis, Sabeans, and Eutychus back to the Catholic faith (letter from Propaganda Fide, September 30, 1826, in NA deposit Iraq in ASV).

locations, and financial aid to poor churches. In October of 1830, Bishop Coupperie asked Rome for a coadjutor and was immediately answered by Pope Gregory XVI who, as a former prefect of Propaganda Fide, well knew the difficulties and problems of the diocese of Baghdad. On June 18, 1831, it was announced that the Vincentian Namanno Falguières Augustine, superior of the priests of the Mission of Naxia, had been named as coadjutor by the pope.

However, before the news could reach Baghdad, Coupperie died unexpectedly on April 25, 1831, during a plague epidemic that decimated the city. The bishop was adamant that Christians not be left to die without the sacraments, and he led by personal example; when one his priests became ill, the bishop cared for him personally, and fell victim to his own apostolic zeal, leaving behind a reputation for holiness, wisdom, and dedication, no less great than that of his predecessor. His death prevented him from dealing with a serious emerging issue that, shortly thereafter, strained relations between Rome and the Chaldean patriarchate: the so-called Malabar question which arose when the Chaldean patriarch of Mosul sought to extend his jurisdiction over Christians of the Syro-Malabar rite in India.

The much esteemed Coupperie was succeeded as bishop of Babylon of the Latins not by Falguières, of whom Coupperie never even received news, but by a new appointee: Fr. Pierre Dominique Marcelin Bonamie (1832–34), of the Picpus Fathers (Congregation of the Sacred Hearts of Jesus and Mary). This new bishop, a native of Albas, near Cahors, was thirty-four at the time, and a professor of theology at the seminary of Tours. He was consecrated bishop at Rome, but, in a sadly familiar fashion, never arrived in Baghdad, resigning for health reasons while on his way to Mesopotamia. Meanwhile, Fr. Laurent Trioche, a colleague of the now deceased Coupperie, wrote repeatedly to Rome illustrating the serious problems that plagued the Chaldean Church, including the massacre of Christians in Alqosh, and the dispute between Augustine Hindi, bishop of Diarbekir—who had been nominated by Chaldean Patriarch Yousuf IV Hindi—and Yohannan Hormidz of Mosul, both candidates for the patriarchate of Babylon. The Holy See, distracted first by the French Revolution and then the Napoleonic occupation of Rome, was unable to give a prompt response or immediately resolve the conflict, which eventually ended with the death of Augustine Hindi and with the recognition of Yohannan VIII Hormizd as patriarch of Babylon of the Chaldeans. With him the two patriarchal lines of Eliya and Yousuf were joined in a single patriarchate based in Mosul. Upon his death in 1838, he was succeed by Nicola I Zaya (1839–46), followed by Yousuf VI Audo (1847–78), a cleric of strong character.

The choice of a successor for Bonamie was not swift; after his resignation, it took three years before Pope Gregory XVI appointed the priest Laurent Trioche, who had been serving as diocesan administrator, as bishop of Babylon of the Latins, administrator *ad beneplacitum* of Isfahan, and apostolic delegate to the Chaldeans on March 22, 1837.[62] Born at Marseilles, Trioche had a good knowledge of Mesopotamia. He had served Bishop Coupperie as his secretary before being ordained a priest, continuing as his closest advisor. As he was raised to serve as his replace-

62. "Delegatum Apostolicum pro Natione Catholica Chaldeorum ... cum facultatibus omnibus necessariis et opportunis ... quando gravius aliquod novum Ecclesiasticum negotium ad exitum perdicendum occurrat" (letter from Propaganda Fide, March 30, 1837, in NA deposit Iraq in ASV). Though the decree was dated March 30, the newly elected bishop only received the news at the end of August. Though surprised by the appointment, he announced himself willing to redouble his efforts for the good of the Church. Like his two predecessors, Trioche was also temporarily placed in charge of representing France (*Histoire de l'Archevêché*, 68), and he received instructions regarding the other apostolic delegates on September 16, 1841. These were similar to the instructions issued in 1839 to the apostolic delegate for Mount Lebanon, M. Vilardell, which consisted of a brief introduction and four summaries on relations with the local Churches.

ment, Trioche referred to himself as an "admirer and faithful follower of [Coupperie]'s on his apostolic journeys since 1820," and now a follower in his pastoral line as well.[63] The papal choice was well-suited for two reasons: first, because Trioche knew the local situation intimately, and had proven as much through several meticulously drafted reports submitted to Propaganda Fide; and second because it was finally recognized that parachuting ill-prepared French bishops—who were unsuited to the difficult and hostile situations they would face and usually lacking in missionary experience—into Mesopotamia was causing more problems than it was solving. In the future, Rome would draw its appointments for Baghdad from those clerics who had lived, or were already living, in the Middle East, thus reducing the risk of candidates who accepted the office but who were reluctant to leave their current home. Moreover, Rome had warmed to the idea of having in place an apostolic delegate, in the person of a Latin bishop, after the positive experiences of bishops Coupperie and Baillet. Ongoing relations with the Chaldean Church, and soon with other ancient Churches of the region as well, now demanded the permanent presence of a papal representative; and Bishop Trioche was the first to officially bear the title of apostolic delegate to the Chaldean Nation.

Upon news of his election, Trioche, received the immediate congratulations of the Chaldean bishops; and he was consecrated in Baghdad on August 15, 1837, by the Chaldean bishop of Gezira, Pier Giorgio di Natale, head of the patriarchal see of Babylon, who was assisted by the Syrian bishop of Mosul Gregory Issa and by the Chaldean patriarch of Babylon Youhannan VIII Hormizd, who came from Mosul for the rite. The occasion drew a large crowd, which followed the ceremony from rooftops, windows,

63. Letter from Trioche addressed to Propaganda Fide, July 17, 1833, in NA deposit Iraq in ASV.

and any possible vantage point. Having the consecration performed by non-Latin bishops aroused considerable admiration and approval for the pope, even among non-Catholics.[64] In the spring of 1838, Trioche undertook a visitation of the Christian villages of upper Mesopotamia, starting from Kirkuk and going to Alqosh: in his report, he noted that the patriarchy was composed of eight ecclesiastical districts, beyond the patriarchal see; and he met other Christian communities in villages further to the northeast. He then visited the monastery of St. Ormisda, staying there for a few days and giving instructions concerning their monastic rule of life. According to him, a major problem facing the Chaldean church was the haphazard training of the clergy, the reform of which he saw as a pressing necessity. Three years later, in 1841, Propaganda Fide took up the issue and began considering the erection of a seminary for priestly formation, and sent Trioche their strong encouragement "to promote it in all his efforts for the benefit of the Chaldean Nation."[65] Thus, in the synod of Chaldean bishops in 1853, the bishops made the proposal a point of special consideration, although they had to wait some time for its establishment. Propaganda Fide, for its part, was also studying how to create in Mesopotamia "a large

64. "Plusieurs m'ont dit que nous sommes a présent convaincus que le souverain pontife honore tous les rites également puis qu'il fait sacrer un évêque latin pour des évêques qui sont d'une autre rit. Qu'elle est belle est heureuse cette église romaine elle réunit tous les peuples dans son sein comme une bonne mère elle les aime tous également, poussions nous un jour nous réunir à elle!" (notes dated August 19, 1837, in NA deposit Iraq in ASV). In truth, the bishop had not been authorized to receive his consecration from non-Latin bishops; but he judged it not only to be an effective gesture but a practical means of avoiding having to make a difficult and hazardous trip to Constantinople to obtain episcopal ordination. The pope then healed, *motu proprio*, the various liturgical and disciplinary irregularities. Beyond the liturgical anomalies, the response of non-Catholics to Trioche's consecration is most interesting, giving us an insight into the positive atmosphere that prevailed among the different Christian communities in Baghdad.

65. Letter from Propaganda Fide, May 3, 1844, in NA deposit Iraq in ASV.

workshop, whose purpose was to educate in the Church, and to instruct in the sacred disciplines of the Latin Church, clerics of the Eastern missions."[66]

Trioche ruled the Latin diocese of Baghdad for about twenty years. He was responsible for the elevation of that see to the rank of archdiocese on August 19, 1848; and he became its first archbishop. He was also appointed apostolic delegate for Persia and represented France as consul in Baghdad. As a shepherd, he consolidated the works initiated by his predecessor, recalling the Carmelites in Baghdad and to whom he entrusted the church and a school for boys; he maintained good relations with the Chaldeans and Assyrians and developed the *sensus ecclesiae catholicae* among all Christians. When he eventually retired from pastoral life, he moved home to Marseille but retained the title of archbishop of Babylon of the Latins until his death on November 27, 1887. During his tenure, in addition to promoting union of the Chaldeans, he championed the cause of Jacobite Bishop Stephen Gezracci, who entered the Catholic faith along with some of his priests. He also supported the missionary commitment of the Capuchins and Dominicans to the Syrians and Chaldean faithful of Mosul and Kurdistan, where they increased conversions throughout the century, and where, in 1847, Fr. Cecchi had founded the monastery of Mar Yacoub. When he returned to Europe, Archbishop Trioche gave up management of Eastern affairs, and Rome appointed the Italian Dominican Merciaj, former prefect of the Mosul mission, to serve as his successor as apostolic delegate. The Latin Church was entrusted to several apostolic administrators: Henri-Marie Amanton, OP; Nicolás Castells, OFM Cap.; Eugène-Louis-Marie Lion, OP; and Henri-Victor Altmayer, OP.

66. Letter from Propaganda Fide, August 5, 1850, in NA deposit Iraq in ASV.

4. The Apostolic Delegation in Mesopotamia, Kurdistan, and Armenia Minor

As a result of conversions among the Nestorians, Jacobites, and Armenians in the provinces of Baghdad, Mosul, and Diarbekir, Bishops Baillet, Coupperie, and Trioche were confronted with the growing spiritual needs of the new converts. As their numbers multiplied, the bishops established or restored bishoprics whose shepherds led their respective communities of the faithful under the authority of the patriarchs. Not infrequently, the apostolic missionaries had to involve themselves in local disputes, and relations between the communities were not always free of misunderstandings and controversies, especially when, in cases of mixed marriages among the faithful, some sought to switch from one rite to another. The Latin bishop of Baghdad was at the center of these cases, which were reserved to the Apostolic See. He insisted on being constantly informed, only granting permissions with caution and for good reason. It seemed proper, therefore, that the matter became the subject of consideration in Rome, covering not only the faithful of Mesopotamia, but also those from other areas of the Middle East. Issues concerning the relations between rites; conversions; the maintaining of communion with the pope by priests, bishops, and patriarchs; and the recognition and relations between the patriarchs and the pope, all began to be taken much more seriously. This was part of a reconsideration of, and a deepening appreciation for, the nature of these Churches which helped increase the recognition of their liturgies and respect for the election criteria of their hierarchy, and influenced Eastern relationships with the Latin missionaries and bishops appointed by the pope, and in particular their roles in relation to the patriarchs.

As relations between the two bodies began to evolve rapidly during the nineteenth century, the Holy See began appointing the first apostolic delegates to different parts of the Ottoman

Empire: first for Syria, Mesopotamia, Kurdistan, and Armenia Minor; and then later for Egypt, Arabia, Turkey, and Persia. The office of apostolic delegate had "become more necessary and more important than a Latin ordinariate"[67] whose faithful had belonged to other Churches from which they had received their baptism, culture, and traditions. So while in the past the bishops and apostolic vicars had represented the Roman pontiff occasionally and under questionable titles (highlighted by the expression *in partibus infidelium*), now, with the new legal form, the delegates were to assume a stable and official capacity, offering Rome the chance to stay informed about the life and development of the local Churches, Catholic and non-Catholic.[68] The first apostolic delegation in the Middle East was established in Syria, with a papal bull, issued on June 17, 1762, and the appointment of Arnoldo Bossù, as apostolic vicar of Aleppo, to whom was given the task of following all the existing Catholic communities in the territory, to whatever rite they belonged, as well as of implementing the papal constitutions and inform the Apostolic See about the life and problems of the Eastern community. The experiment was repeated in Mesopotamia with Trioche, who was appointed delegate for the Chaldean Nation, and then Constantinople and Persia. But the establishment of the apostolic delegates was not without problems; the Turkish government, while not ignoring their existence (the delegate of Constantinople was accepted as a channel of communication between the pope and the sultan), did not recognize their work

67. *Histoire de l'Archevêché*, 69–70.

68. It is possible to trace the evolution from the origins of these apostolic vicars and bishops *in partibus* to the modern delegations: "Especially the Latin bishops and apostolic vicars of the Ottoman Empire, constituted by the popes to correspond with those persons invested with the supreme civil power, to start, continue, and sometimes to complete work directed toward the conversion of the leaders of schismatic churches and their followers, and to inquire after the status of the Catholic Church" (D. Bracket, *Catholic Encyclopedia* [Vatican City: 1950], s.v. "Executive Officer Apostolic Annex").

with, or jurisdiction over, Catholics who were Ottoman subjects. The authorities did, however, formally recognize certain bishops, giving them the right to issue administrative orders affecting members of their Churches.[69] The delicate position of the delegates meant that they, even in religious matters, had to tread very carefully, so as not to offend sensibilities or raise create unnecessary conflict which could draw in the Turkish authorities. This explains why the French embassy at the Sublime Porte became, until the time of the collapse of the Ottoman Empire, the preferred means of relaying protests and demands in the interests of the Latin Church. When Henri-Victor Altmayer (papal representative for eighteen years in Mosul, from 1884 to 1902) wanted to better explain his role as papal delegate, his outline for the role, while similar to a description of delegates in other places, emphasized the particular circumstances of the situation of Mesopotamia Christianity. He claimed that the apostolic delegate was not, properly speaking, a foreigner, but was instead fully in the community and the events, "happy and unhappy," which marked the "progress, struggles, and sufferings" of the life of the local Churches, while simultaneously serving as

Guardian of the authority of the Holy See and possessor of its solicitude, necessary overseer of all that touches the faith and discipline, counselor of the patriarchs and bishops, president of the synods or of those whom they elect, confidant and advocate of the needs the dioceses, and channel of subsidies that it intended for pious associations, the promoter of the apostolate among the heretics, benefactor of the clergy, refuge for Christians in the unhappy day of trial; the apostolic delegate is not foreign to any act of life of these Churches, always ready to encourage and assist in the good, careful to set aside

69. This legal issue was at the center of a dispute between the apostolic delegate Nicolás Castells and the Armenian bishop Nazarian, who opposed the apostolic delegation to the schismatic church (see letter dated August 10, 1872, from the consulate of France in Aleppo to Castells, in NA deposit Iraq in ASV).

or heal the sick. Pope Leo XIII defined the role of this ecclesiastical official in a single word in its constitution of November 3, 1894, as the "conciliator."[70]

Through the presence of these apostolic delegations in their respective territories, the pope himself was placed at the service of the Eastern Churches as the stone upon which to build an edifice of fidelity and unity among all Christians with Christ. He was also more closely informedly about the life of these Churches, and could better show them his concern, sending them pastoral and financial support, together with the more important and solemn acts of the Petrine ministry, and, in some severe cases, he could urge more delicate diplomatic action through those governments with more influence at the Sublime Porte. It should be noted that France, through her ambassador and her consuls, showed great willingness to use her influence at court in favor of the Mesopotamia delegation, aware that the foundation of the Latin diocese of Baghdad was due to the generosity of a French noblewoman and in consideration of the fact that its incumbents were French and, not infrequently, consuls themselves. At the time of the Restoration, France resumed her geopolitical interest in Mesopotamia, forming a three-sided axis (Mosul, Baghdad, and Basra), not only to control British activities in the region, but also to defend her own influence and extend her protection to the Christians of the region.[71]

70. *Histoire de l'Archevêché*, 71–2.
71. "Il est indispensabile d'en concilier l'exercice [the protection of the Christians of the Ottoman Empire] avec prudence et les ménagements que comportent, non seulement les droits de souveraineté et d'administration de la Porte sur ses sujets, mais encore les difficultés que l'éloignement des lieux oppose nécessairement à l'action de l'Ambas- sade du Roi et à celle de la Porte elle-même" (P. de Vaucelles, *La vie en Irak il y a un siècle* [Paris: A. Pedone, 1963], 6, also 89–92, on the protection of Christians; and 102–107, on the reports of French consuls in their Iraqi colonies). The author notes that the Restoration government was very sparing in its financial support, despite having entrusted the protection of French interests in Baghdad to

At this point, the apostolic delegation in Mesopotamia, Kurdistan, and Armenia Minor included most of the territories of the Chaldean and Syrian patriarchates and some Armenian dioceses. It was a large territory which ran from the present borders of Syria, to southern Turkey, to Azerbaijan; and it extended throughout modern Iraq. The Chaldean patriarchate was, at this point, comprised of nine bishoprics, one hundred sixty secular and religious priests, and about forty thousand faithful; the Syro-Catholic patriarchate of Antioch had five bishoprics, eighty priests, and about twelve thousand faithful; finally, the Armenian Catholics occupied the region between Trabzon, Malatya (Melitene), and the upper Euphrates, consisting of five dioceses, forty priests, and about ten thousand faithful.[72] Also working within the territory were French Discalced Carmelites (Baghdad and Basra), the Dominicans (first Italians and then the French in Mosul, Mar Yacoub, and Kurdistan), the Capuchins (Spanish and Italian in Mardin, Orfa, Diarbekir, and Seert), and finally, the Jesuits and the Vincentians toward Persia. The good that they worked is vividly attested to in a letter of the Syrian-Catholic archbishop of Mosul, Cyrille Behnam Benni, dated July 28, 1870, which extolled their presence and apostolic activity, and especially the commendable zeal which they lavished on educational and social works.[73]

the apostolic delegate, never granting any remuneration, except on very rare occasions.

72. The delegate Altmayer records that, existing in this territory of two patriarchates, 17 bishops, 300 priests and 65,000 faithful, "l'archevêché latin de Bagdad ... , a eu sa grande et belle part dans la création et la diffusion du mouvement catholique en ces contrées" (see *Histoire de l'Archevêché*, 76).

73. *Les Missions catholiques* 3 [1870]: 57–59.

5. The Case of Reversurus and Vatican Council I, the Chaldean Patriarchate versus Rome, and the Malabar Affair

With Pius IX (1846–78), the papacy was shorn of the demands of temporal governance; and, freed from such secular cares, it was able to focus on the Church's spiritual mission, and on evangelization and reform. At this time in the Church's history, a providential host of saints and scholars would give a great impetus to ecclesiastical life, and to the missions among the pagans, which aroused a great enthusiasm among the people of God; while, at the same time, the Church began to dream of a true union of all Christians in her dealings with the Orthodox Churches.[74]

The early years of development in missionary work took place in the countries of the Near East, that is, those closest to traditionally Christian lands. During this time, the Church was studying the concept of missionary work as it was carried out in different ways and forms. Following a long evaluation, Pius IX, with the apostolic constitution *Romani pontifices* (January 6, 1862) created a division within Propaganda Fide between missionary work *pro Gentibus* and those whose mission which were *pro Orientalibus*, creating a separate section Pro negotiis ritus

---

74. "The bull *Ecclesiam Christi* (November 26, 1853) formed the general principle of unity in diversity," writes Giacomo Martina, and "is similar to the position outlined by Benedict XIV"; however, "the bull did not address the real underlying problem. Was the characteristic of diversity in the Church limited to differences of language and rite, or did it admit to a theological-ecclesiological pluralism?" "In conclusion the thrust of Pius IX's policy toward the East, in this period, up to 1864, can be summed up in these essential features: bitterness about the controversy with the Orthodox, respect for the traditions of the Eastern Rite Catholics, the absence of an examination of the possibility of an ecclesiological pluralism, lack of energy to enforce obedience by those missionaries likely to Latinize Orientals" (Giacomo Martina, *Pio IX (1851–1866)*, vol. 51 [Rome: Gregorian University Press, 1986], 362–63).

orientalis, which, while sharing the same cardinal-prefect with the rest of Propaganda Fide, had its own archbishop-secretary, consultants, and officials.[75] This reform was part of a more general process of reform to be undertaken across the Eastern Churches, about whom there was a growing uneasiness concerning their administrative and ecclesiastical practices. With the apostolic letter *Amantissimus* (1863), the pope asked for an in-depth study of the state of the Eastern Churches, believing that their bishops and clergy had succumbed to a culture of mediocrity and authoritarianism in patriarchal and diocesan governance, and that pastoral initiatives had completely dried up in the face of clerical squabbling and venality. For these and other reasons, the pontiff, with the bull *Reversurus* (July 12, 1867), decided to regulate the election of bishops in the Eastern patriarchates, starting with the Armenians and Greek-Melkites,

75. Sacred Congregation for the Eastern Churches, *Oriente Cattolico*, 12; Lesourd, *Histoire des missions catholiques*, 116. According to Giacomo Martina (*Pio IX*, 368): "The erection of the Special Section of Propaganda Fide ... showed positive intent. It demonstrated the interest that Pius IX had for the Catholics of the various Eastern rites" and reiterated "the will of the Holy See to respect the non-Latin rites" (368); he goes on to note: "The interest of Pius IX for the Oriental Churches had been apparent since January of 1848 with the letter *In suprema Petri apostolici sede*. Since then, his work in this field had expanded; the founding, in 1862, of a special section of Propaganda Fide for Eastern Rite issues constituted the culmination of a long ongoing process. The principle that inspired the action of the Holy See was clear: respect for the rituals and traditions of the East" (359); for Martina, in fact, "the popes had never claimed to Latinize Orientals, their sole concern, as Benedict XIV declared in his constitution *Allatae sunt* of 1755, that they remain unchanged and free of errors" (366). Yet there were cases of converts (former heretics or schismatics) who tied their conversion to Catholicism with admission to the Latin Rite; for these cases, Pius IX wanted the Section for Eastern Affairs of Propaganda Fide to establish "a general rule to be followed in such circumstances," and granted to delegates and apostolic vicars the five-year faculty to dispense, "perpetually and absolutely," the transition into the Latin rite, if the one seeking the transfer was in a true real state of necessity (doc. 10, July 31, 1665, in NA deposit Iraq in ASV; Pius IX approved the statutes on June 17, 1865).

but proposing to eventually extend the same reforms to the other patriarchates, including the Chaldeans.[76] The pope wanted to leave the patriarchs some time to digest his intentions and, hopefully, to inspire them with "the initiative to reform this important point in ecclesiastical discipline."[77] The Chaldean patriarch Audo seemed to accept the idea of reform without too much difficulty.[78] Soon afterward, on August 31, 1869, the pre-

76. Letter from Propaganda Fide, dated November 15, 1867, in NA deposit Iraq in ASV.

77. Letter from Propaganda Fide, dated August 20, 1869, in NA deposit Iraq in ASV: Alessandro Cardinal Barnabò, prefect of Propaganda Fide, wrote to the apostolic delegate of Mesopotamia, Nicola Castells, in which he told him he was: "sending (to the Armenian Patriarch Harcus) a copy of the Consistorial Acts relating to the election of the Armenian patriarch, and the constitution *Reversurus*, I informed him of His Holiness's intention to similarly reform the election of bishops in other the patriarchates; and expressed my hope that he would receive the decisions of the Holy Father with the same docility he had always shown to the Holy See. This letter (sent from Rome on February 24, 1869) remains unanswered at this point ... they know well that the Holy See recognizes the need to regulate the election of prelates in the Eastern patriarchates, and that the intention is to extend the measures contained in the above-mentioned constitution *Reversurus* to everyone. The spirit of moderation of the Holy See has previously challenged the individual patriarchs on this point and they are now left to take the lead in this important work of reform of ecclesiastical discipline."

78. On July 31, 1868, Audo had written to the pope concerning the regulations for the election of bishops: "We indeed wished for these provisions... and others designed to reorganize the whole Eastern Church and which could produce canons useful for all situations" (Martina, *Pio IX*, 96–97). Cardinal Barnabò was alluding to this and other reports when he wrote: "His Holiness has told me how meekly the Chaldean Patriarch Mgr. Audo has welcomed them from when he was first sent the constitution. I could not believe that Mgr. Harcus (Syrian Patriarch of Antioch) met with difficulties from him. Therefore the best way [of proceeding] would appear to be by using the proximity of that prelate, and the esteem he has for you, to encourage him to strive with all prudence in the indicated direction; and to ensure that all of you have the same desired response; this would be all the more welcome, as it will be more attentive and explicit" (Letter from Propaganda Fide, dated August 20, 1869, in NA deposit Iraq in ASV). About the particular dissension in the Chaldean Church, see Martina, *Pio IX*, 96 and following.

fect of Propaganda Fide wrote that Pius IX "was well convinced of his excellent disposition toward the Holy See, of which his last letters have given especially singular proof, he does not believe there to be any lingering opposition to the enactment of appropriate measures in the patriarchate to codify the election of prelates, along similar lines to what has already been established for the Armenian patriarchate"; he then added: "In this way the Holy Father wished to establish the fundamental basis of the reorganization of ecclesiastical discipline, of which the Chaldean patriarchate had so much need, and which His Holiness still ardently desired, as he has made known to me in other letters." Declaring that they wished to follow a more intermediate course of reform, somewhere between a radical overhaul of patriarchal traditions and leaving them untouched, Rome sent Audo the apostolic letter *Cum ecclesiastica disciplina* (August 31, 1869), which extended to the norms of *Reversus* to the Chaldean Church.[79] But the new law sparked resentment and dissent, first within the Chaldean Church, and then between the pope and the patriarch, whose relationship was marked by serious tensions which lasted for a decade; beginning with an argument over episcopal provision of the dioceses of Diarbekir and Mardin,[80] followed by Audo's nonadherence to the concil-

79. Letter from Cardinal Barnabò, prefect of Propaganda Fide, to Patriarch Audo, dated August 31, 1869. In it he noted that "the rest will be most usefully explained, in person, here in Rome [where the patriarch intended to go to participate in the First Vatican Council, which opened on December 8, 1869]; for I am sure you will travel here with all of your bishops, as the Holy Father strongly desires." It should be noted that the envelope containing the papal document was returned to Rome because of a postage error; given that the patriarch was already on his way from Mosul to Rome, the letter was handed over to the Capuchin Zechariah Catignano for urgent delivery. For the text of the apostolic letter *Cum ecclesiastica disciplina*, see ASS 5 (1869–70), 637–643.

80. The pope had elected two priests, Farso Gabriel and Pierre Attar, to serve as bishops of these dioceses. Their names were taken from a list of suitable clergy drawn up by Audo, who then contested their appointment anyway (letter of Propaganda Fide, March 24, 1869, in NA deposit Iraq in ASV).

iar constitution *Pastor aeternus*,[81] and then the vexed Malabar question.

In those years, the contagion of the new liberal ideologies was causing international political, religious, and social turmoil. Even the Church was not immune from the effects of the post-Enlightenment revolutions, which attacked her faith, discipline, and authority. Pius IX, to stem the tide, decided to promulgate, on December 8, 1864, the encyclical *Quanta cura* and the *Syllabus of Errors*.[82] It was in view of the "great and grave evils, so unfortunate in the times we live in, afflicting the Catholic Church and civil society through the antireligious and antisocial doctrines, ranging everywhere and spreading with immense damage to the good of souls ... not only in Western countries, but also in those of the East," the pope decided to convoke a council,[83] following discrete consultation with his delegates and closest associates, who were supposed to report "with brevity and accuracy, the errors, abuses, and other spiritual needs, and which, in the main,... they would agree to provide."[84]

The celebration of Vatican Council I (1869–70) represented the greatest ecclesiastical event of the pontificate of Pius IX and was the way the Catholic Church, as a whole, sought to respond to the challenges, both external and internal, posed by the world. He wanted the council to be doctrinal in its response to the liberal and secularizing tendencies of the time; but also

81. Patriarch Audo actually left Rome early to avoid signing the document.

82. Although these matters were not as pressing in the East, Rome asked the pro-delegate, a Capuchin named Nicola Castells (called Nicola da Barcellona), to send the documents to all the bishops so they could publish their contents (letters from Propaganda Fide, dated March 31, and September 15, 1865; in NA deposit Iraq in ASV).

83. Pius IX, bull *Aeterni Patris*, June 29, 1868.

84. Letter from Propaganda Fide, February 22, 1866, in NA deposit Iraq in ASV.

ecumenical,[85] inviting the participation of "each and every schismatic prelate, of whatever rite, dwelling within the area of the Mesopotamian delegation."[86] The council was also intended to give a renewed impetus to the missionary activity of the Church, including in the ancient Christian lands. Propaganda Fide took responsibility for this and began a project of great importance, which would have no small effect in Mesopotamia. It was at this time that schools and educational establishments were erected in all the dioceses of the Church. These were intended to lift the poorest of society out of religious and cultural ignorance and to counter the further encroachment of Protestantism. Alessandro Cardinal Barnabò, lamenting that the Mesopotamian delegation "does not have a sufficient number of Catholic schools" in its territory, informed the Capuchin Nicola da Barcellona, apostolic pro-delegate, that Propaganda Fide had decided "to contribute to the erection of Catholic schools in the places which need them most, by administering, at least for some years, a certain amount." At the same time, he asked to "know the number of schools that would be more necessary in the delegation's area, the places in which it would agree to establish them, and what the annual amount for each of them should be."[87] This project was a welcome gift to the people of the villages, who saw it as the answer to many of their prayers. The schools continued up until the era of the Iraqi government, which eventually succeeded

85. Pius IX, apostolic letter *Arcana divina providentia*, September 8, 1868.

86. So wrote Alessandro Cardinal Barnabò to the apostolic delegate Nicola Castells (letter of Propaganda Fide, September 28, 1868, in NA deposit Iraq in ASV). As the opening session approached, the Apostolic See persuaded the French government to provide free transportation, through their Navy, for all French bishops who wished to use it; so too did the shipping company Österreichischer Lloyd and the Atlantic and Indian Ocean Lines (letter of Propaganda Fide, June 8, 1869, in NA deposit Iraq in ASV).

87. Letter from Propaganda Fide, April 25, 1866, in NA deposit Iraq in ASV.

the Ottoman Empire, and the policy of nationalization for private schools. The Dominicans of Mosul had already anticipated the new policy from Rome, opening a school in the city, as had the previous apostolic delegates Planchet and Amanton in the Christian villages, all of which met with success. According to a report from Nicola da Barcellona submitted to Propaganda Fide, those populations most in need of primary school places were the Chaldean villages; at the same time, he noted that the biggest problems were stoking the desire to establish them, and assisting them in finding suitable teachers.

The first man to receive the title of apostolic delegate for Mesopotamia, Kurdistan, and Armenia Minor, was the Dominican Antonino Merciaj (1849–50), former prefect of the mission in Mosul, and a native of the province of Siena (Italy). He was consecrated archbishop on January 28, 1849, and given the titular see of Theodosiopolis, but died suddenly in Diarbekir, where he had established his residence. Following the sudden death of Merciaj, the Holy See appointed the French Jesuit Benoît Planchet (1851–59), of Beirut, as "pro-delegate." At that time, Planchet was in Gazir, where he had spent some considerable time as an apostolic missionary. He was well known for his zeal, his experience, and his knowledge of the local language and customs. His instructions told him to make contact with the Chaldean bishops of Seert and Cattula, Bishop Basil of Gezira, and the Chaldean patriarch Audo. He was also instructed to immediately see to the vacant diocese of Amadia. The new pro-delegate traveled extensively between Beirut, Aleppo, Mardin, and Mosul, where he lived for long intervals. He had many sensitive issues to deal with, including a request from the Syrian-Jacobite patriarch, along with two of his bishops, to enter ecclesiastical communion with Rome, as well as handling the conversion to Catholicism of some Nestorian priests, despite the Ottoman government's official opposition to such conversions.

In January of 1852, Planchet was appointed to lead the Chaldean synod and to favor the election of Ignazio Antonio Samhiri as a new Syriac Catholic patriarch. On June 15, 1853, Pope Pius IX confirmed Planchet in his role, in which he had served for more than two years with zeal and satisfaction, appointing him apostolic delegate and titular archbishop of Trajanopoli. From December 1853 to January 1854, as an extraordinary delegate, Planchet presided over the Syrian Catholic synod at Charfet (Lebanon), which he directed with care, leading it to the election of Samhiri as the new patriarch, who was also confirmed by Pius IX on March 18, 1854. In October of the same year, Planchet was also required to preside over the work of the Chaldean synod, following tensions between the bishops and the patriarch.[88] Rome recommended that Planchet attend only as an "observer," but this did not stop him reporting back to Propaganda Fide that the problems of the Church were rooted in the poor training of the clergy. Following this, Propaganda Fide began to push for the opening of a seminary to provide a better theological, spiritual, and cultural formation for the clergy; they also began preparations to open a printing house to publish texts for training and for popular devotion. Another area of emphasis for Planchet was developing the women religious apostolate. In a land devoid of religious congregations, he understood that the presence of a congregation of women would be of enormous benefit; and he had the support of Rome. He was also responsible for trying to mitigate the fallout of Kurdish uprisings, which took a violent toll on the Christian community. He encouraged France, which still wished to strengthen its presence in the area and to act as a guardian of Christian minorities, to open consul-

88. The Jesuit Badour said that with that synod Planchet had joined the Chaldean bishops "more strongly than ever, as the center of Catholic unity" (*Annales de la Propagation*, vol. 30 [1858], 330, b). But this attitude gave rise to accusations of attempting to Latinize ecclesiastical institutions and was one of the greatest problems under Patriarch Yousuf IV Audo.

ates in Antioch, Orfa, and Diarbekir, through which they gathered intelligence and pressured the local Ottoman authorities—often indifferent to the protection of the rights of minorities—to act. Unexpectedly, in November of 1859, while on the dangerous road from Orfa to Suérek, Planchet was attacked by robbers and died from his injuries.

Meanwhile, in 1856, the French province of the Order of Preachers had agreed to take over the mission of Mosul, which had been run by the Italian Dominicans for nearly a century, and to make it the center of its activities in the heart of Mesopotamia. By the arrival of Father Besson, considerable bonds had been forged between Mosul, the Dominicans, and France, which also appointed a vice-consul who became almost the formal guardian of the mission. In this new context, the Dominican Marie-Henri Amanton, from Dijon, was designated to replace Planchet. Amanton had been in Mosul for about three years, initially arriving to replace Father Agostino Brands, apostolic prefect of the Italian Dominican mission, where he was to become bishop of Arcadiopoli *in partibus*, apostolic delegate for Persia and apostolic administrator of Baghdad of the Latins from 1857 to 1864 (Archbishop Trioche, although he had withdrawn from the office, still retained the episcopal title). Shortly thereafter, he was also appointed apostolic delegate for Mesopotamia, Kurdistan, and Armenia Minor (1859) combining the delegations of Persia and Mesopotamia. In the course of his short tenure, Amanton moved the seat of the delegation to the Dominican residence in Mosul, because "l'affaire du Malabar," as he used bitterly to call it, required his presence there. Poor health, however, soon compelled him to return to France, where he died, aged forty-six, on October 12, 1869. His office was entrusted to the Spanish Capuchin Nicola Castells, also called Nicola da Barcellona, who served as pro-delegate from 1865 to 1873. Shortly thereafter, in July of 1866, he was elected archbishop of Marzianopoli, administrator of Baghdad and apostolic delegate for Persia, Mesopotamia, Kurdistan, and Armenia Minor. The prelate, sixty-six years old, chose to take up residence in Mardin, not only because he was familiar with the place, but also because its central location allowed freer contact across the vast territory entrusted to him. Unfortunately, in the late spring of 1868, Castells suffered from apoplexy, which prevented him from fully engaging with his work. In looking after the pastoral life of the diocese of Baghdad, he relied upon the prefect of the Carmelite mission, Father Marie-Joseph de Jésus; and he made almost no use of his office as delegate for Persia, whose functions would be transferred to the bishop of Isfahan in 1872. The weightier matters, which Castells had to deal with personally, concerned the internal situations of the local Churches, including the election of a new Syrian patriarch of Antioch, following the death of Samhiri, and seeing to the succession of the Armenian Patriarch Gregory Peter VIII, as well as trying to settle the problems caused by the papal bull *Reversurus* and the apostolic letter *Commissum* (July 4, 1867), with which Pius IX regulated the unification of two Armenian-Catholic sees: the patriarchal see of Cilicia and the primate of Constantinople, the latter of which was extinguished, causing opposition between the clergy and the faithful, ending in schism.[89] It also involved Patriarch Audo, who was part of the controversial reception of Vatican Council I, centering on *Pastor aeternus*. Audo had left Rome

89. The bull *Reversurus* (ASS 3 [1867]) extended restrictions that had previously been applied to the primatial see of Constantinople to the Armenian Catholic Patriarchate of Cilicia. These including the requirement of the synod presenting a *turns* of three candidates from which the Holy See would choose the patriarch. These would be changed, *perpetuis futuris temporibus*, by Pope Leo XIII, who recognized the synod of bishops' right of election, with the obligation to ensure the canonical suitability of the candidate. *Reversurus* caused an enormous backlash, including the deposition of Patriarch Adon Bedros IX Hassoun, and the election of an antipatriarch. This schism was not healed until April 18, 1879.

without participating in the last session of the council (*Schema constitutionis dogmaticae de Ecclesia Christi*) or taking part in the vote. To avoid expressing his opinions openly, Audo gave out that the reason he left was to consult his people. In fact, he was against the constitution itself, though the other Chaldean bishops present at the council accepted the document.[90] The patriarch's protest greatly alarmed the prefect of Propaganda Fide, who tried to recall him by appealing to his sense of Catholic duty and principles. Relations with Rome, were beginning to fray, especially after the appointment of Timothy Attar and Gabriel Farso as bishops of Diarbekir and Mardin. These two had received papal approval, having been elected by the Chaldean synod and the patriarch himself, but Audo now he refused to consecrate them, without offering any serious reasons.[91] The aftermath of the affair remained a lingering concern for Rome, and fed the growth of schismatic voices. In view of the seriousness of the situation, and given Castells's poor health, Pius IX decided to give him "help, all the more urgent for the insistent efforts of the enemies of the Church to sabotage Catholic unity in these parts."[92] The choice fell on the Capuchin Zaccaria da

90. The final draft of the *schema* was approved during the last general session of the congregation (July 16), it was decided that the public session would be held on July 18. Fifty-two council fathers, including Patriarch Audo, left Rome before the vote; the dogmatic constitution (*Pastor aeternus*) was approved with the consent of the 535 bishops who were present.

91. The relevant reforms were approved by Pius IX in the apostolic letter *Cum ecclesiastica disciplina* on August 31, 1869 (*ASS* 5 [1869–70], 637–643). The document regulated the appointment of the patriarch, stated that only bishops could participate in the synod and forbade the immediate enthronement of anyone elected without the prior confirmation of the Roman pontiff and the conferral of the pallium. As to the appointment of bishops, the synod chose three candidates who were proposed to the pope, who selected the one most suitable for the vacant see. See also Martina, *Pio IX*, 96 and following.

92. Letter of Propaganda Fide dated November 20, 1871, in NA deposit Iraq in ASV.

Catignano (whose born name was Fanciulli), then prefect of the Franciscan mission in Beirut. He was appointed bishop of Maronea *in partibus* on November 24, 1871, and, at the same time, also was named as extraordinary apostolic delegate for Mesopotamia, Kurdistan, and Armenia Minor.[93] His instructions required him to travel as soon as possible to Mosul, where they urgently needed his presence and mediation. The dispute with Patriarch Audo had entered a new stage, with his resumption of the never formally renounced Chaldean aspiration of extending jurisdiction over the Malabar Church. He now began sending Chaldean bishops there, in violation of direct papal orders not to interfere with the Malabars.[94]

Fanciulli's immediate priority was to get to Mosul, obtain Audo's acceptance of the council, and dissuade him from his intentions toward the Malabar Church. The new pro-delegate actually managed to get the patriarch to sign a declaration claiming to fully accept Vatican Council I, and specifically the dogmatic definition of the infallibility of the Roman pontiff on matters of faith and morals when he teaches as pope and head of the Catholic Church.[95] Great indeed was Pius IX's satisfac-

93. Fanciulli was well known in Lebanon for his zeal, sweetness of disposition, and prudence. He was born on April 7, 1812, at Catignano (Abruzzo); he entered the Capuchins at fifteen and was ordained a priest in 1835. In 1841 he left as a missionary for Syria; in Beirut, he became assistant curate of the Latin community. In 1856 he was appointed apostolic prefect of the Capuchins of Syria and later pro-vicar general of the Latin patriarch of Jerusalem. He was consecrated bishop on February 18, 1872, by the Latin patriarch of Jerusalem Giuseppe Valerga (1847–72).

94. Propaganda Fide had already made clear their thoughts on the subject in letters dated May 21, 1864, and May 23, 1865, in NA deposit Iraq in ASV.

95. According to the Dominican Pietro Gonzalez Duval, pro-prefect of the apostolic mission of Mosul, the repentance of the patriarch and his acceptance the council was in part the work of the French consul, Bernard Lanusse, a prudent man and devoted to the Holy See. But the patriarch's acceptance was far from full, he had reservations, which resurfaced in 1874 when he proceeded to illicitly ordain bishops. The prefect of Propaganda

Fide responded with a letter dated August 27, 1874, in which he stated that Audo's reservations would be "well-considered," and would be rejected if they "had to recognize a limitation of the dogmatic Vatican definition, which is an absolute condition to which he must adhere. But it is also to be considered that you declared in the same act to have always been devoted since childhood to the Holy See, and to have always, with great tenacity, adhered to all that the Holy Roman Church teaches and orders; and that accordingly you felt compelled to manifest that which had always been in your heart, though only expressed later, for good reasons.... So it was decided that such a reservation was motivated by a direct desire to decrease the irritation that your act of acceptance was likely to produce in that district, for it was and is troubled, rather than to limit your statement of faith, which otherwise would have been illusory, indeed absolutely contradictory. It was because of this that His Holiness wished to proceed with the greatest possible mercy toward you, and attributed this meaning to the act, for it was both logical at the time and Catholic; and in this sense only he accepted it. And for greater caution and clarity he does not omit to remind you of the divine order of the hierarchy established by Jesus Christ as a result of which the Roman pontiff has the right and duty to regulate, as best as he judges beneficial to the salvation of souls, the powers and privileges lawfully enjoyed by the major offices, all of which are derived from St. Peter and his successors. It is therefore not true that the Holy Father, in receiving the above-mentioned act of acceptance, has accepted the proposed reservations, and it is far less than what he could do, or would seem inclined toward doing, as all would have easily have been made aware, had your act elicited the aforementioned papal response. It is even said that you believed that the Holy See has promised to you the granting of Malabar; and that these and other promises have been made in Mosul by those who have worked to get you to fulfill the strict obligation of conscience that is required of you expressly to declare your adherence to the decrees and your submission to the ecumenical council. Now it cannot be believed that you would allude to such promises, which more than once were asserted before the resolution of the Sacred Congregation on March 23, 1865, and in that case it referred back to the letter of that the same Holy Congregation, written on May 21, 1864, when they freely denied such assertions. As for statements and promises you claim were made to you by other means, especially when you performed the inescapable duty to profess your adherence to the dogmatic constitutions of the Ecumenical Vatican Council, I can assure you, that the Sacred Congregation has never given commission or permission to let you conceive any such hopes, especially in regard to Malabar, or the election of bishops. And if it were true, which I cannot believe, that Mgr. Fanciulli has made such promises or given similar hopes, he certainly would have far exceeded the mandate he received from the Holy See: for this reason we will not confirm what these, or any others, may have wantonly promised or caused you to hope. Surely you could not

tion, and he answered with a beautiful letter, dated November 16, 1872, in which, among other things, he asked for a positive resolution for the provision for the see of Diarbekir and condemnation of the Armenian schism. This satisfaction then was confirmed by the prefect of Propaganda Fide (September 30, 1873), which informed the patriarch of the Holy See's consideration of the Malabar question and confirmed their view, while urging him to help overcome the Armenian schism and prevent Ottoman governmental interference in doctrinal disputes between the Armenian faithful and Rome. In the spring of 1873 Fanciulli went to visit Baghdad and Amara (near Basra). It had been a very long time since a Latin ordinary had inspected the Carmelite missions, and the faithful joyfully welcomed him everywhere he went.

By this time, the Servantes de Dieu—the women's religious congregation founded by Coupperie—had succumbed to the problems constantly besetting them and were now extinct. So, in their stead, Fanciulli began to think about inviting in a foreign institution, and he contacted the Dominican Congregation of the Sisters of Charity of the Presentation of the Blessed Virgin of Tours (known as the Dominican Sisters of the Presentation). The sisters arrived at Mosul in the fall of 1873 and assumed the work of catechesis, school education, and health care for abandoned children.

On September 3, 1873, while still hard at work, the apostolic delegate Nicola Castells died; only the day before he had been urging the Armenians to begin a revival movement and had ordained several new priests. His funeral saw the participation of Catholics, Orthodox, and Turks, proof of the esteem he

---

conceive of such enticements, after we have repeatedly and clearly written to you to oppose any designs on Malabar, and asked you to instead look after the good of your own patriarchy; this Sacred Congregation repeats this again to you today and confirms it peremptorily" (letter from Propaganda Fide dated April 13, 1872, in NA deposit Iraq in ASV).

enjoyed, and of the apostolic mission which drove him in his many works at Mardin over the years. It was widely assumed that Fanciulli would simply continue his work without interruption, but a few weeks later, he too died unexpectedly at Mardin on November 4, 1873.

In December 1873, not without some surprise, Pius IX appointed the French Dominican Eugène-Louis-Marie Lion as archbishop of Damietta *in partibus*, and apostolic delegate of Mesopotamia, Kurdistan, and Armenia Minor; and Latin administrator of Baghdad (1873–83). The papal brief urged him to assume his new office as quickly as he could, and instructed him about the mission which lay ahead, and in particular the case of the Chaldean Patriarch Audo. The new delegate had been a missionary in Mosul for twelve years, and he held the office of pro-prefect of the Dominican mission. He had left an indelible memory of his pastoral zeal as an educator and popularizer of religious literature through the religious press.[96] When he had been recalled to France his departure had been much regretted by the local community, and so there was considerable surprise and satisfaction when the Holy See announced him as Castells's successor. But the new delegate had a difficult situation to contend with from the moment he arrived in Mesopotamia.[97] The

96. The printing house was a very popular initiative, publishing hagiographic, devotional, and catechetical works for the Chaldeans and Syrians. In addition, he proposed to print a correct edition of the New Testament in Arabic, "Une Bible vraiment catholique, dit le R. P. Lion, est indispensable dans ce pays, où les fideles n'ont d'autre version entre les mains que des Bibles protestantes cells" (*Les Missions catholiques*, vol. 3 [1870], 124). The Bible was printed in 1875 and reprinted in 2002, on the occasion of the 250th anniversary of the installation of the Dominicans in Iraq.

97. He recalled a letter written by his friend Vogue, French ambassador to Constantinople, May 2, 1874: "You cannot doubt with what satisfaction I learned of your appointment as apostolic delegate for Mesopotamia. The memories that you left the country, the service that the order to which you belong renders every day, everything recommends the choice of the Holy See … [who can] count on your knowledge of the country, on the wisdom of

Turkish government had embarked on "a campaign against Catholicism, the more fanciful than right, with the apparent rationale being the defense of the rights of Catholics, or so they claim."[98] The problems, in fact, came mainly from within the church, but they found willing ears in the politics of the Ottoman Empire, so much so that Pope Pius IX had to issue new disciplinary norms, especially regarding the election of pastors. Even before Lion arrived in Mesopotamia, Patriarch Audo took advantage of the absence of the delegate to plan the ordination of four bishops (two religious and two secular) and to send some to Malabar, in open violation of the provisions of the Holy See which, at the news, expressed more sorrow than surprise.[99] Lion did not depart for Mesopotamia immediately after his episcopal consecration as he had been directed to by Propaganda Fide.

---

your spirit, no less than on your apostolic virtues, to impart to the journey of religious affairs a happy direction; you must not ignore the threat of the Malabar question, which can still give problems, such as in the succession of the Syrian patriarch. The example given by the Armenians, and inextricable complications introduced by the promulgation of the bull *Reversurus*, are felt in these regions, and the ill will of the Ottoman government is against all that is faithfully Catholic, which only adds to the difficulty of the situation. You will know better than anyone how to take all this into account, and it is very necessary that you impart some measure of prudence to the ecclesiastical authorities. The reports of the apostolic delegates concerning the Ottoman Catholics are not simple reading: the Ottoman government has been induced to take their part; they have been drawn in by the native Catholics whose clergy suffer the disciplinary supervision of the delegates, through their instigation they have begun to consider, and will perhaps soon ask, what exactly is the situation of those prelates who have neither the function nor jurisdiction of a bishop-ordinary, nor formal diplomatic character, yet by right exercise authority over Ottoman subjects, in some cases with civil effects; so under no circumstances give occasion to raise this matter, as the current circumstances are not favorable." Letter from Propaganda Fide, May 2, 1874, in NA deposit Iraq in ASV.

98. Letter from Propaganda Fide dated May 26, 1874, in NA deposit Iraq in ASV.

99. Audo had been urged on by some of his clergy, including the superior of the monastery of St. Ormisda and Bishop Elijah Mellus.

Indeed he probably had no clear knowledge of the events and maintained an ambiguous attitude on the Malabar issue.[100] Cardinal Franchi, prefect of Propaganda Fide, intervened, and, given the worsening of the crisis, he spoke directly to Audo, reminding him of the noble intentions he had expressed in the past for the apostolic see and the pope's will; he also reminded him of the serious penalties he would incur if he sent his own bishops to Malabar.[101] Nevertheless, Audo proceeded to send Bishops Mellus and Barthatar, who left immediately for Malabar. Despite the warnings, the patriarch announced a further episcopal ordination, which took place in Alqosh. Pius IX wrote in person to the patriarch, keeping a patient tone, and invited him to consider the good of the Church, but he also gave powers to the apostolic delegate to intervene with censures, and even to depose Audo should the patriarch continue on his course.[102] In response, the patriarch denounced Rome to the vizier in

100. The French Embassy in Constantinople had directed the concerns voiced in Mosul to Rome, "The patriarch wishes to ordain two religious as archbishops [Mattei and Bolous] and two more as priests [Ilo and Alphonso], though they hesitate. One archbishop is bound for Malabar. Archbishop Elia and the religious superior are the leaders of this movement. This is a matter of great urgency. He [Lion] must see that the consecration of bishops would be in open opposition to the apostolic constitution *Cum ecclesiastica*; and that the designation of a Chaldean bishop for Malabar would be contrary to the very well-known dispositions of the Holy See, of which the Holy Father has already ordered the full observance." See letters from Propaganda Fide dated June 5, 1874; and June 25, 1874, in NA deposit Iraq in ASV.

101. Letters from Propaganda Fide dated August 27, 1874, in NA deposit Iraq in ASV; Two separate letters were sent, on the same date, to the two priests (Elia Mellus and Matteo Barthatar), who had been illicitly consecrated as bishops for Malabar. The letters declared their consecrations to be "illegitimate and sacrilegious" and their mission from the patriarch to be "null and void." The now schismatic Mellus and Barthatar undertook the journey to Malabar. They were preceded by a letter to the apostolic representatives there (dated on the feast of St. Peter in Chains, 1874), in which they were instructed not to receive Mellus and Barthatar, and informed of a penalty of excommunication for those who did.

102. Pius IX, apostolic letter *Inter ea*, March 17, 1876.

Constantinople,[103] declaring himself a subject of the sultan and calling for action against the apostolic delegate, the missionaries, the French consulate, and the clergy faithful to the pope. Then, in a letter dated from Alqosh on March 19, 1876, Audo wrote Pius IX a very long letter in which, professing his catholicity, he tried to explain away his actions and complained that his intentions had been distorted. He further alleged that he had been the victim of malicious accusations and that he, together with the Chaldean people, had suffered greatly at the hands of the missionaries. The letter served to offset the Latin complaints against the patriarch; consequently, the charges and penalties of *Inter ea* were suspended, and the whole matter put out for further study. On September 1, 1876, Pius IX sent the Chaldean patriarch and the faithful a letter titled *Quae in patriarchatu*, in which he laid out the facts of the matter and exhorted all to Catholic obedience. The patriarch was given forty days' notice, after which he would be excommunicated;[104] the apostolic delegate was given the power to appoint new administrators for those places lacking legitimate pastors. Upon receipt of the papal letter, Audo declared on March 1, 1877, that he submitted to the authority of the pope, along with the vast majority of the clergy and the faithful; and he recalled the emissaries sent to Malabar. Lion informed the pope of Audo's change of heart by telegram on March 4, and Rome received the news with relief. Yet some of the bishops among Audo's supporters resisted the submission to Rome and split from the patriarch. They excommunicated Audo themselves and elected an antipatriarch named Ciriaco Zakho. While they expected government support for their rebellion, the Ottoman government, acting through Mustafa Pasha (a Jewish apostate to Islam and the governor of Mosul), grudgingly deposed Ciriaco, dealing a serious blow to the schismatic wing.

103. The political-religious adviser to the sultan.
104. *ASS* 10 (1877), 11–37. See also Martina, *Pio IX*, 104–5.

Given the new situation, Lion and the patriarch were ordered to recover the schismatics and restore some degree of normalcy in ecclesiastical life; and relations between Rome and the patriarchate began to improve steadily.

On February 7, 1878, Pius IX died. Despite the many disappointments that life had reserved for him, Providence at least had spared him a Chaldean schism. He was succeeded on February 20 by Pope Leo XIII, who appointed Cardinal Franchi as his secretary of state and right hand. French was himself succeeded as prefect of Propaganda Fide by Cardinal Simeoni. Shortly thereafter, on March 29, the now-reconciled Audo died at Mosul as an "obedient son of the Holy Catholic Church, in submission to the Holy See."[105] While the schismatic Ciriaco tried to profit from the interregnum, the government of the Sublime Porte, despite the clear anti-Catholic sympathies of Mustafa Pasha, recognized Timothy Attar, archbishop of Mardin, as patriarchal administrator, at the recommendation of the apostolic delegate Lion.

The synod of Alqosh met in July 1878 and was chaired by the delegate with the authority he had been granted by the Apostolic See. The body unanimously elected as the new patriarch Boutros Eliya VI Abolionan VI (1879–94), bishop of Gezira; and the choice was approved by Pope Leo XIII in the consistory of February 28, 1879. The new patriarch immediately sought to improve relations with Rome, which, in 1882, lifted the censures and rehabilitated three illicitly consecrated bishops and several illicitly ordained priests. Bishop Mellus, however, did not give up his schismatic intrigues and did not amended his ways toward the end of his life.

The Mesopotamian delegation also had to deal with the Armenian schism, which had also taken place within the Ottoman Empire, and which brought no less painful divisions to the Church. After the civil emancipation of the Armenian Catholics

105. Martina, *Pio IX*, 107.

granted by the Sublime Porte through the Treaty of Adrianople (1829), Pius VIII had created the primatial see of Constantinople (July 6, 1830), notwithstanding the existence of the patriarchal see of Cilicia, which had been erected on March 26, 1740. The patriarchal see, though more historic and prominent, was, in practical matters, now under the primate, who was officially recognized by the Sultan. On July 12, 1867, the synod of Bzommar elected Adon Bedros IX Hassoun as the new patriarch; and a few months later (July 1867), with the bull *Reversurus*, Pius IX unified the patriarchal and primatial offices, with Hassoun receiving the pallium at first and then the imperial *bérat*.

At this time, the patriarchate of Cilicia consisted of seventeen bishoprics, and the persecutions of the previous century seemed a distant memory; but the reform of episcopal elections, introduced by *Reversurus*, and then the decrees of the Vatican council, inflamed tempers toward schism. A breakaway faction elected Hagop Bahtiaren as antipatriarch. He was succeeded by Ohan Kupelian, who was favored by the Ottoman authorities who do not care for the close relationship between the Hassoun (himself an Ottoman subject) and the Roman pontiff. The schismatic struggles took place mostly in Armenia Minor and in Turkish lands, where local governors never missed a chance to promote the schismatic group against those faithful in Rome. The French ambassador in Constantinople, who had the informal role of defender of the Christians, could not always protect them on his own, and, not infrequently, even the British and Austrian ambassadors had to intervene with the Turkish government. The fight between the two factions continued with increasing ferocity until Leo XIII agreed to mitigate some of the reforms of *Reversurus*: Kupelian then recanted and was pardoned on April 18, 1879. Hassoun was made a cardinal, and the Ottoman government changed its attitude toward the Catholic Church from open hostility to tolerance. The apostolic delegates for Constantinople and

Armenia Minor were asked by Rome to work toward returning the protestors to full communion and asked the Jesuits to undertake the mending of the rift across all of Armenia.

Meanwhile, having received the red hat in December of 1880, the faithful Cardinal Hassoun left Constantinople for Rome, where he would represent the East in the College of Cardinals. Since Kupelian had made an act of submission to Leo XIII and was back in the Catholic communion, it seemed appropriate that the Armenian Church chose a new leader. This took place on July 7, 1881, and Stepanos Azarian, archbishop of Nicosia, became the new patriarch, taking the name of Stepanos Bedros X Azarian (1881–99).

In the postconciliar storm that enveloped the Armenians and Chaldeans, the Syro-Antiochian archbishop of Mosul, Behnam Benni, remained steadfast in his fidelity to the Catholic Church, resisting pressure from Mustafa Pasha, who threatened to depose him. Benni and his clergy were not afraid of Ottoman intimidation and were willing to face all the ensuing difficulties they received for their loyalty to Catholic principles. This worthy prelate suffered greatly from Jacobite conspirators who, strengthened by the government, tried to wrestle away possession of half of his churches, all of which had been closed since 1876. In 1878 the bishop decided to go to Constantinople in person to defend their rights against the Jacobite claims, and to complain about the blatantly anti-Catholic conduct of the pasha and the negligence of the Sublime Porte in defending the legitimate rights of his people. He managed to be received by the highest echelons of government, including the prime minister, who was under continuous pressure from the governments of France, Austria, and Great Britain. In truth, it was not only Archbishop Benni who was on the receiving end of the Ottomans' anti-Catholicism. The Syriac patriarch Ignace Georges V Schelhot had been refused the imperial *bérat* since his election, on the pretext that he had accepted *Reversurus* and the council. But neither the patriarch nor his bishops would yield to civil pressure, and, in June of 1875, he was eventually granted the *bérat*. Despite these difficulties, the Syrian Catholic Church had the considerable consolation of the conversion of hundreds of monophysite families who had lost their sense of faith and Christian morality. Their numbers were so great that, in September 1862, the Syrian Catholic diocese of Baghdad was erected and led by Bishop Athanasius Raphael Jarghi, who built the first churches for that rite in the city.

The complex and tortuous events that took place between the apostolic delegation and the Chaldean patriarchate had made clear the need to give the delegation its own official residence and office, separate from the Dominican convent where it had been based. After short intervals at Diarbekir and Mardin, the Dominican house in Mosul had been selected as the sight, rather than Baghdad, because of the city's location between Mesopotamia, Armenia Minor, and Kurdistan. Mosul was actually the ideal place for the apostolic delegate to reside; the city had a large, mixed community of Christians, it was the crossroads for southern Mesopotamia, and it was an important civil, commercial, and missionary center. But the close Dominican association was itself no longer tenable since, from the moment Patriarch Audo had complained to Rome about the Dominicans, they were at the center of the opposition to the Chaldean Church. Therefore, in 1876, Lion suggested that Propaganda Fide build a separate residence. The Vatican dicastery quickly agreed to the proposal, thinking the measure "entirely useful and certainly necessary."[106] Despite some problems raised by the Ottoman authorities, by the time of Lion's death, the new building was almost complete.

106. Letter from Propaganda Fide dated January 20, 1876, in NA deposit Iraq in ASV.

Simultaneously, another work was under way that was just as important: the establishment of an inter-ritual seminary for training clergy. After a failed attempt to create such a seminary in the Chaldean monastery of St. George, not far from Mosul, in 1853, the project was shelved. On March 23, 1865, Alessandro Cardinal Barnabò wrote to Patriarch Audo that it was necessary for him to open a seminary for the good of his Church, and, a few days later, he also wrote to Nicolas Castells, then pro-delegate, asking him to erect, as soon as possible, a seminary for the education of the clergy under the authority of the apostolic delegate, and to evaluate the feasibility of erecting two: one papal and one patriarchal. After twenty-two years of study and expectation, on January 10, 1878, the project of an inter-ritual seminary for the Chaldeans and the Syrians was approved. On September 7, 1882, Propaganda Fide formally erected the institution, entrusting it to the Dominicans, under the authority and jurisdiction of the delegate for Mesopotamia, and named for the Saints John the Evangelist and Thomas Aquinas.[107] For nearly a century it would play a highly commendable role in forming priests for the Eastern Churches, until its closure after Vatican II.

Lion did not neglect his role as administrator of Baghdad, nor ignore the needs of the Latin Church in that city, which he visited several times, seeing to the needs with the Carmelites in Bagdad and Basra, the Dominicans in Mosul, and the Capuchins and Jesuits in Mardin, Orfa, and Diarbekir. To provide better pastoral care to women and girls in Baghdad, in 1880 he brought in the Dominican Sisters of the Presentation, who had

107. The seminary became known as the Seminary of St. John. At that time Mosul was also home to the small Chaldean patriarchal seminary of St. Peter, founded in 1865, which was usually home to five or six seminarians, and which the new patriarch wanted to expand. It continued to exist even after the erection of the Syro-Chaldean seminary. The new seminary's charter (given on September 7, 1882) was approved *ad experimentum* for ten years, as was its mission, methods of education, direction, etc.

already been present in Mosul since 1873, and to whom he entrusted the reorganization of education for poor girls, and the establishment of schools, kindergartens, and clinics. To support the educational projects, both for boys and girls, Lion relied upon the support of various benefactors, including the French government, which made generous donations, given the interests of France in Mesopotamia. In the social field, a hospital was founded in Mosul, thanks to a pious French noblewoman, the Baroness Lejeune, who donated of fifty thousand francs for the project, believing it would serve as a vital tool and support for missionary work in the city.

In those same years, from 1877 a local congregation of women religious became part of the ecclesiastical scene of Mosul: the Dominican Sisters of St. Catherine of Siena, known as Caterinettes, which were started by the desire of three lay Dominicans, and supported by the Dominican fathers. During his tenure, Lion gave threw his full support behind the missionary impulse recommended by Leo XIII, and he saw many schismatics embrace Catholicism, as was the case with the entire village of Deh. He visited the Baghdad community, the Capuchin mission of Mardin, and the churches of Kurdistan and Armenia Minor (Alqosh, Mar Yacoub, Zakho, Diarbekir, Orfa); and, on his way to Constantinople, he took the opportunity monitor the situation in Malatia (Melitene), where a church had been burned down because of the conversion of eighty families, and to visit Karpouth, where a good number of Armenian villages had joined the Catholic faith. In September of the same year, he met the new Armenian Catholic patriarch Stepanos Budros X Azarian in Constantinople, and discussed with him the best way to increase conversions and to beat back the influence of Protestantism among the good and simple Christian population. He stayed in the Ottoman capital for a few months and then, in December of 1881, he left for Rome to make his *ad limina* visit in his capacity as Latin administrator of Baghdad. He returned to Mesopotamia and died unexpectedly at Alqosh on August 8, 1883, at the cave-monastery of St. Ormisda, where he had sought shelter from the summer heat which had brought on serious health problems. He was buried in the chapel of the Cave of the Virgin, where there is still a plaque in his memory.

Archbishop Lion was a good man, faithful to his vocation and to his office; he was greatly mourned by the people and by the Chaldean patriarch, who recognized his efforts in ending the schism and bringing about a new Catholic unity among the faithful.

Meanwhile, Leo XIII (1878–1903), sensing the changing times and new political and ecclesiastical developments, anticipated a reshaping of relations with the Eastern Churches through his important apostolic letters *Praeclara gratulationis*[108] and *Orientalium dignitas*.[109] He could foresee an end to the era of the Latin missions in the Middle East, as he was increasingly honing a whole new approach to the ancient Churches and wanted to eliminate the lingering Latinizing impression left by the very concept of the missions. He thought it far more appropriate in lands of first evangelization, to trust in the well-established pres-

108. Given on June 20, 1894, on the occasion of his episcopal jubilee. In it, Pope Leo XIII expounded upon the need to strive for the unity of all Christians and gave assurances that the Holy See would respect the rights and privileges of the other patriarchs, as well as the liturgical customs of their Churches (*ASS* 26 [1893–94], 705–17). The pontiff also consigned *Reversurus* to history and finally closed the painful chapter it had authored.

109. Given on November 30, 1894, Leo XIII recognized the legitimacy of the Eastern ecclesiastical jurisdictions, as well as their full dignity and guaranteed respect for their liturgical traditions: "The venerable antiquity that characterizes the different types of oriental rite is an excellent source of pride for the whole Church and reveals the divine unity of the Catholic Church" (*ASS* 27 [1894–95], 257–64). Also he invited the patriarchs, Catholic and non-Catholic, to converse with him in Rome to promote union; the project was sadly ill-fated, because the Orthodox rejected the premise of a "return" to the Catholic Church.

ence of Churches in communion with Rome (Chaldean, Syrian, Armenian, Greek, Coptic) and to increasingly give over to them the process of communion with the Orthodox Churches. He decided, therefore, that all pastoral care of Eastern Christians held by a Latin was to be returned to the proper Churches as a sign of renewed respect for the local hierarchies and to mark a new era in relations between the Churches.[110] Then, with the motu proprio *Auspicia rerum*,[111] the pope turned the full force of his own personal solicitude toward the Christian East, and gave precise instructions for stirring up among the people to zeal for the faith and for its former glory, as well as for strengthening their union with the See of Peter and promoting the reconciliation of dissidents. The document's intention, which is to say the intention of the pope himself, was to complement *Orientalium dignitas* while reaffirming the role of the Roman pontiff's delegates as advocates of Catholic unity, and, at the same time, executors and interpreters of the will of the pope. He asked the delegates to be facilitators, along with the patriarchs, of a spirit of concord. As to the patriarchs, Leo XIII reaffirmed his respect for their dignity and authority, and wrote: "We wish ... that the patriarchs have a spirit of fraternal trust in Our delegates ... in order to treat the most important questions with common accord." He urged them to meet together at least twice a year, while reaffirming the right of the same patriarchs to set up, manage, and develop their own seminaries, for which he promised to provide not only financial support but, if necessary, staff.[112]

110. Letter from Propaganda Fide dated March 9, 1895, in NA deposit Iraq in ASV.

111. Given on March 19, 1896 (*ASS* 28 [1895–96], 585–90).

112. The Syro-Chaldean seminary of St. John in Mosul, directed by the Dominicans, welcomed the new address and called new staff, so that there be at least one priest of every ritual of the students, so as to "celebrate Mass and fulfill the other works prescribed by the aforementioned constitution ... [as] suitable means to pave the way for the application of the constitution itself without spiritual damage to the Syrian and Chaldean faithful ... in

Another key point to which the pope called attention was the multiplication and support of schools for the education of children, and all of God's people, and the publication of newspapers and periodicals so that explanation and discussion of doctrine and the truth could be in regular circulation among them. The pope also touched upon the issue of relations between the delegates and the *missio sui iuris*, insisting that the superiors have a spirit of obedience toward his representatives and did not embark upon important initiatives without their approval. Also of significance were the instructions issued to the delegates: they were to guard and provide for the application of *Orientalium dignitas*, and to work to completely eradicate the impression that the Latins wanted to make an attempt to usurp the rights, privileges, or liturgical traditions of the Eastern Churches. They were instructed to assist the missionaries with their good council and persuade them, when appropriate, of the great importance of living in unity and friendship with the local clergy.

In this context, there was a clear need for the establishment of an "Apostolic Delegate for the Conversion of the Nestorians" in Mesopotamia, and that this should be the Chaldean patriarch.[113] The prefect of Propaganda Fide, Cardinal Ledòchowski, also issued instructions giving "the means by which the missionaries should proceed for the evangelization of the Nestorians." The cardinal recommended that, though they acted with the good intention of bringing them back to the Catholic faith, they must not organize them as "a part of that people in a Catholic community separate from the other [Chaldeans]." Indeed, he insisted that "this policy be abandoned" and that, in the work of conversion, they pursue only those who sought conversion for

---

that city and in other churches or chapels of the Dominican mission within the territory of the apostolic prefecture" (letter from Propaganda Fide, no. 3473/16, dated April 23, 1895, in NA deposit Iraq in ASV).

113. Leo XIII, apostolic letter *Ad sinum*, July 31, 1902.

"truly religious and supernatural motives." Finally, he reiterated the importance of the clergy in maintaining ecclesiastical discipline, giving catechesis for the people, and establishing primary schools, and most of all in ensuring that these works proceed in all "harmony and peace."[114]

114. The full text of the document merits reproduction here, since it illustrates the new ecclesiastical landscape as desired by the pope: "Although the well-deserving Dominican fathers have worked with zeal and holy diligence with the intention of returning Nestorian people to the Catholic Church, the results have been unhappy, because their burning desire to achieve this coveted goal has prompted some of them to use less than appropriate means, especially the intention of organizing a part of that people into Catholic communities separate from the others [Chaldeans]. It is the desire of the Holy See that this conduct be abandoned; and it is now ordered that the fine work for the conversion of Nestorians follow these instructions:

1. Missionaries should refrain from making political promises, or attempting to satisfy temporal ambitions or interests, which are foreign to their religious ministry.

2. Converts must not be accepted if they affix conditions to their conversion or manifest earthly needs, or if there be even a suspicion of political aims or interests; but it should be required of them that they present definite proof that they are motivated by truly religious and supernatural motives.

3. The immediate aim of all missionaries, Latin and Eastern, must be to dispel the darkness of ignorance among the clergy and people of the Nestorians concerning dogmatic, moral, ritual, and sacramental matters; showing them the errors they have professed to date and the truths of the Catholic religion; and at the same time endeavoring to rehabilitate their customs and to implement among them the practicalities of truly Catholic life, and organize at least the basic structure of Catholic worship.

4. To that end, missionaries should employ the methods used throughout the Church, that is: continued preaching, adapted to the intellectual capacity of the listeners; teaching catechism; establishing elementary schools; distributing suitable Catholic pamphlets and similar materials.

5. Schools are to be entrusted to Catholic teachers zealous and above any question in their religious or moral probity; and, as frequently as possible, they are to be visited and carefully inspected by the missionaries, so that nothing is taught there that is not fully compliant with the holiness of the Catholic faith, and that they maintain perfect purity in their customs.

6. The missionaries must work with zeal and prudence to cement, as best they can, concord and peace.

7. Again we enjoin the observance of previous instructions on the subject, and especially those contained in the letter of this Sacred Congregation

Lion's office now being vacant, Giovanni Cardinal Simeoni, prefect of Propaganda Fide, sent a letter, dated March 22, 1884, informing the Dominican Henri-Victor Altmayer that Pope Leo XIII had appointed him apostolic delegate for Mesopotamia, Kurdistan, and Armenia Minor, and apostolic administrator of Baghdad of the Latins, with the title archbishop of Halkida.[115] On November 27, 1887, following the death of Archbishop Trioche, he also became archbishop of Baghdad of the Latins. The new prelate left Mosul for Rome and then carried on to Metz, where he received his episcopal consecration on August 10, together with the Légion d'honneur[116] from the French government. He then returned to Mosul, where he was warmly received by the church authorities and the French consul. Altmayer, like his predecessor, resided in Mosul, where he completed construction of the delegation headquarters, located next to the inter-ritual seminary, while the pastoral needs of the community in Baghdad continued to be looked after by the Carmelites, who had enlarged their church and their school for boys. The Carmelites also purchased a new site for the archbishopric

to Msgr. Enrico Altmayer, apostolic delegate for Mesopotamia dated January 10, 1893, no. 1664/2."

M. Card. Ledòchowski, prefect; Ant. Savelli-Spinola, secretary (letter from Propaganda Fide dated January 10, 1902, in NA deposit Iraq in ASV).

115. Letter from Propaganda Fide dated March 22, 1884, in NA deposit Iraq in ASV. Altmayer was born at Metz; after a military career, he became a missionary at the age of 28, departing for Mesopotamia, in 1874, to serve in Lion's delegation. He served as a faithful and attentive secretary, acquiring knowledge and experience in Church affairs. Lion had considerable confidence in him, entrusting him with special tasks (in 1879 he was put in charge of the development of social and educational works in Baghdad) and the administration of the delegation during his absences. It should be noted that the episcopal title assigned to Altmayer did not include the sobriquet *in partibus infidelium*; Leo XIII had changed this practice in the public consistory of March 30, 1882, in consideration of the fact that the ancient titular sees were often inhabited by Christian populations (*Les Missions catholiques*, vol. 14 [1882], 172).

116. This is the highest civil honor awarded by the French Government.

itself, with the church and the parish next to the girls' school run by the Dominican Sisters of the Presentation.[117] Both orders were sustained by the regular assistance of the French government, which Rome had reconfirmed (1888) as the protectorate of the Christians of the East.[118] The Ottoman government had indeed often created obstacles for the schools, including those in Baghdad, making it one of the major points of contention with Paris and causing a crisis of mutual diplomatic relations. The matter was only finally resolved in November 1901, when Constantinople legally recognized the existence of the schools, finally acknowledged the work of religious hospitals by exempting them from taxes and customs fees, and authorized the construction and repair of buildings being used for educational or social work. Other Catholic institutions had enjoyed similar discrimination, including the Latin archbishopric in Baghdad, as well as the religious communities and Latin Churches of Basra.[119] Socially and educationally, great efforts had been made to meet the problems of widespread poverty and illiteracy; but in the pastoral field something much more daring was needed to address the general religious ignorance among Christians. Altmayer realized that a greater and more constant presence of the bishop was needed in order to study, encourage, and provide better for the missionary needs; but the large size of the

117. Between 1885 and 1890, Altmayer brought first five, then ten, and then fifteen Dominican Sisters of the Presentation across from France to help develop the educational institutions. The sisters taught French, music, Arabic, and various handicrafts. The orphanage housed girls either without parents or who had been abandoned. By 1899 the kindergarten, school, and orphanage was home to 800 girls. The nuns also ran a Third Order and an association for young people.

118. Letter from Propaganda Fide dated June 2, 1897, in NA deposit Iraq in ASV. On January 21, 1898, Altmayer informed the French ambassador in Constantinople. France claimed this right because of the three centuries of French missionary presence in Mesopotamia.

119. Office of the ambassador of France to the Sublime Porte, November 21, 1901.

territory and the various difficulties of the region prevented him being everywhere at once. In November 1897 he requested that Rome send him an auxiliary bishop permanently to look after Upper Mesopotamia, where political and ethnic turmoil were an ever-present reality. He believed that the presence of a personal representative in that region would help the evangelization there and allow him to deal more calmly with other serious tasks that were constantly demanding his attention. Rome was initially favorable to the idea, but, because of the difficulty of finding a suitable candidate and fearing that the precarious political and religious balance would be upset by the appointment of a new Latin bishop, they preferred to postpone it; the plan was then definitively shelved in November 1899, because, wrote Cardinal Ledòchowski, of the "complexity of the present circumstances."[120]

Altmayer devoted particular attention both to his pastoral mission, and to his role as apostolic delegate. For the latter role, his priorities remained: the improvement of relations with the Catholic Churches of different rites; the training of clergy, with a special focus on the Syrian-Chaldean seminary of St. John; education for poor children in Baghdad, Mosul, and Basra; and the reopening of the Carmelite missions in Basra and Amara. He also encouraged a strong religious sensibility among the Christian population through catechetical instruction and the dissemination of popular devotions and, in deference to the spirituality of the time, he obtained recognition of the Sacred Heart of Jesus as a patron of the Latin Church from the Congregation of Rites. This devotion was widely accepted by the local Christian families of all rites.

Altmayer took to heart the difficult economic conditions of the Syrian and Chaldean dioceses, whose needs he knew only

120. Letter from Propaganda Fide, no. 10392/39, dated November 13, 1899, in NA deposit Iraq in ASV.

too well; and he often acted as their advocate in Rome, as had Lion before him, at Propaganda Fide. Across his territory, he never failed to encourage the local authorities to intervene when Ottoman law threatened the protection of church property. And he tirelessly encouraged the bishops to work to end, or make less burdensome, the sad situation of the Christian peoples of Mesopotamia brought on by political, economic, and religious oppression. This was particularly acute in the small Christian villages of the Kurdish regions, which were at the mercy of fanatical intolerance, violent raids by bandits, and the constant ineptitude and injustice of the aghas,[121] all of which only got worse during the frequent political struggles and famines. There is extensive correspondence and reports from these dioceses from the Chaldean monk Geremia Makdassi and from Yousuf Emmanuel Thomas, who, having just arrived in Seert as bishop, referred to it as "this miserable city" and "this, my poor and abandoned diocese" in a letter dated October 30, 1892. He also reports that on January 16, 1897, in Békiend (Cazas Gharzan), a married Chaldean priest named Petros was murdered, along with his son, and his wife, daughter-in-law, and grandson were all seriously wounded, by members of the Risso tribe, who were Kurdish thieves and looters. On October 21, 1897, the prelate wrote to Altmayer again, informing him that the village of Beingof was not only "looted" but "completely destroyed," adding: "It impossible that this diocese can live long, if the conditions remain the same as they are today." On September 26, 1902, in a dramatic letter, the patriarchal vicar of Seert, Thomas Bajari, lamented the endless violence of some Kurdish tribes, whom no one dared to punish.

In the short span of a decade, the diocese of Seert declined dramatically and eventually disappeared; its Christians migrating mostly either to Europe or Iraq. It was situations like this that gave Altmayer such a personal concern for the Chaldean

121. *Agha* was a Turkish title for a local civil and military lord.

Church and inspired him to work ever harder to overcome the consequences of the schism of Bishop Mellus, reorganize the religious life at the monastery of St. Ormisda, and inspire an increase in popular piety. As he continued his work, he deeply appreciated the assistance of the patriarch Eliya XIV Abolionan (1878–94), who, over six years of collaboration, helped to pacify and resolve many issues.[122] He was succeeded, for a brief period, by Giorgio Ebed-Jesu (also called Audishu) V Khayyat (1894–99), who was elected by a synod chaired, at the request of Rome, by Altmayer, despite attempted Ottoman interference. The Holy See provided that, should the Chaldean clergy try to intervene in the appointment process, Altmayer could try to avoid greater disruption and ask them for the names of five or six candidates from which the synod would elect the new patriarch.

Meanwhile, the normalization process of the monastery of St. Ormisda, which had been undermined by decades of internal disputes, departures, and divisions, turned out to be rather more delicate and complex than expected. Altmayer managed to make a canonical visitation in 1892 with Patriarch Abolonian, whom he wanted directly involved. Altmayer was adamant that the supreme authority of the Chaldean Church had to take responsibility for the influence the monks exercised in his Church.

Altmayer also considered it part of his role as delegate to help develop the spiritual and cultural life of the clergy and the faithful. Improving its content was one of the challenges that were outlined for the Church, and he championed any initiative which favored its development, including getting the Vincentian Father Begjan in Rome to print a Chaldean breviary to encour-

122. Letter from Propaganda Fide to Patriarch Eliya XIV Abolionan, prot. no. 1, March 21, 1884. See also prot. no. 680/15, of April 24, 1889, in NA deposit Iraq in ASV, which describes a group of Chaldean dissidents, aided by the Armenian patriarch Stepanos Bedros X Azarian, who continued to agitate for the repeal of the constitution *Cum ecclesiastica* and petition the Ottoman authorities for a settlement more in their favor.

age daily prayer among the clergy, and arranging the publication of a version of the Bible, called the Peshitta, for the Dominicans of Mosul, as well as a Chaldean translation of the catechism of Trent and a new edition of the missal for the liturgical care of Chaldean parishes. His tenure saw many conversions from the Nestorians, Armenians, and Syrian Orthodox; and these were mostly because of the work of the Dominican missions, who had, in Fr. Galland, a formidable and tireless promoter. These conversions included some especially noteworthy successes, including Nemroud, who was a close relative of the Nestorian Patriarch Shimon XVIII, and even the Armenian Orthodox Archbishop Pio Battista Dikraniant, who converted with one hundred Armenian-Eutyches families from Bachkalé. In addition to these, dozens of families converted in the villages of Kurdistan, and, in Medeat, two hundred Syrian-Orthodox families converted to Catholicism under Bishop Julius Benham of Gezira.[123]

In the autumn of 1900, Altmayer left for Europe while formally remaining in charge of the work of the delegation, but he resigned in May 1902, citing health reasons, and went to live in Paris, taking the title of archbishop of Sinnade.[124] Before leaving for Europe, Altmayer had participated in the election of a new Chaldean patriarch, a process which was complicated by the interference of the Turkish government, who refused to recognize the synod after they were excluded from its deliberations. The feverish consultations between Cardinal Rampolla, who was the Vatican secretary of state, and the French government, which still maintained the protection of the missions, only served to

123. The Syrian-Catholic patriarchate in Mesopotamia at this time had five bishops, eighty priests, and twelve thousand faithful, and was led first by Patriarch Scelhot until 1891, then by Cyril Behnam Benni until 1897, and then by Ignatius Ephrem II Rahmani, who was an active and prudent man, who transferred the patriarchal seat from Mardin to Beirut.

124. A Dominican named Goormachtigh served as interim administrator of the delegation and of the archdiocese.

make the Ottoman authorities more stubborn; and the affair clouded relations between Paris and Constantinople. Eventually, the Chaldean bishops, firmly supported by the apostolic delegate, addressed a formal declaration to the *valy*[125] of Mosul rejecting the civil claims to be involved. They held a synod in July 1900 and elected Yousuf VI Emmanuel Thomas, bishop of Seert and a great friend of Altmayer, as patriarch; he would serve from 1900 to 1947.

The presence of the delegate at the synod was a contentious event: the Ottoman government demanded that the Chaldean episcopate make a declaration that he had been present only for prayers and had not been present for the business of the synod; a demand clearly detrimental to the freedom of the Church which the bishops bluntly rejected. The government interference and attempts to control religious minorities was a political response from Constantinople to the nationalist turmoil of the time—it had worked in other instances such as in the resounding election of the Armenian Catholic Patriarch Boghos Bedros XI Emmanuelian, following the death of Azarian, when Constantinople demanded that, before the election, the synod present a list of bishops over which they would exercise a veto; a demand which the synod submitted to out of fear.

In eighteen years of service to the Church of Mesopotamia, Kurdistan, and Armenia Minor, Altmayer followed in the footsteps of his predecessor, Lion, completing and developing the initiatives that they had started together. Before submitting his resignation, the outgoing delegate presented the pope with his assessment of the problems afflicting the Church and the apostolic delegation, and which considered as major "obstacles to the progress of Catholicism." These included the impression that some prelates looked to union with Rome more for privileges out of vanity and pride; poor cooperation between the Catholic

125. The civil authority of the city.

communities; the increasingly miserable plight of Christians in the Ottoman Empire; and, finally, the lack of care by the clergy because of episcopate inaction.[126]

On November 7, 1902, Pope Leo XIII appointed a new bishop for the vacant See of Baghdad of the Latins—a French Carmelite from the province of Avignon, Jean de la Sainte Famille, also called François Désiré Jean Drure, who had been a missionary in Basra since 1883. He was welcomed into Baghdad joyfully by the clergy and people. The following year, on March 5, 1904, Pope Pius X appointed him apostolic delegate of Mesopotamia, Kurdistan, and Armenia Minor as well. The new bishop then went to reside in Mosul, where he was again greeted with sympathy and honor during a difficult time for the dioceses of Upper Mesopotamia.[127] With his accession, the apostolic delegation passed from the hands of a Dominican to those of a Carmelite, by which Rome hoped to have a healthy turnover of ideas and experiences. Aware of the deficiencies and needs of the Mesopotamian churches, Drure interceded for the various dioceses, making appeals to Rome, and procured the liturgical books and pastoral materials so necessary for the spiritual life of

126. In a letter written in Rome and dated February 25, 1901, concerning the fourth "evil," Altmayer said that it consisted of the "plethora of priests who neglect their duties because of poor organization and poor management." He added: "Without patrimony or pay, they have to think first of all to survive and sustain their families, making it their first and foremost goal."

127. The bishop of Seert, Addai Scheer, descried the miserable condition of Christians that became daily more desperate and drove the community to an inexorable exodus. On March 16, 1905, the bishop wrote to Drure: "The Chaldean Catholics are about 600 families. Most, if not all, are in a miserable state; I say this without exaggeration: it is clear that as the dioceses that are located in Kurdistan are the most miserable of all the dioceses of the East, so the diocese of Seert is the most miserable of all the dioceses of Kurdistan." In its report of November 14, 1906, the bishop noted: "My diocese, as I have said, will soon be deserted. Recent events in Armenia have seen thirteen villages destroyed or occupied by the Kurds ... all the fields are occupied by Muslims ... my diocese is in agony" (in NA deposit Iraq in ASV).

the local communities. He ensured he followed a very collaborative approach to the Chaldean Church, knowing that Patriarch Youseph VI Emmanuel Thomas was a loyal ally to the pope and devoted to his nation, and a man who governed his Church well, overseeing his priests and maintaining good relations with all.

After visiting the Chaldean dioceses of Mosul, Amadia, Zakho, and Seert in the spring of 1905, the new delegate outlined to Rome the innumerable difficulties the local Christians were facing and reiterated the request for help in securing their basic needs. The local Christians were victims of massacres and looting, as in the case of the Armenian Catholics of Bittlis, deprived of religious assistance, and subject to endemic poverty. There were complaints against the Armenian priests of Mardin, and against Syrian priest as well, which were sent to Patriarch Rahmani. Armenian families from the village of Kujlu left for Georgia because of a total lack of priests. One of the major complaints concerned the monastery of St. Ormisda. The synod and the patriarch complained to Rome about the decadence of their religious life and Propaganda Fide, in principle, accepted their requests and decided to declare null and void the recent admission of thirty young men, because they did not meet the norms established on December 4, 1899. The whole situation aroused misgivings, and Propaganda Fide asked the patriarch to express his opinion. He proposed separating the novices from the senior monks and establishing a new novitiate in Alqosh, thereby extending the mandate of the abbot general. Rome approved and extended the position of the abbot *ad triennium*, provided that he was supported by specially selected moderators. Rome agreed to the appointment of a new director of novices and asked for news about the thirty suspended religious. The whole painful episode lasted ten years and was eventually closed with a general amnesty on September 9, 1909.[128]

128. Letter from Propaganda Fide to Patriarch Yousuf VI Emmanuel

The Syro-Chaldean seminary in Mosul, however, directed by the Dominicans and under the protection of the apostolic delegate, was going well; the pupils' progress was encouraging, and in its more than twenty years of operation it had borne considerable fruit. For this reason, Propaganda Fide decided to provide it with permanent status and a *curriculum studii* in philosophy, theology, and canon law. In 1914 the seminary was closed because of the war and the subsequent persecutions. They had instructed 190 pupils, twelve of whom (eight Chaldeans and four Syrians) offered their lives in fidelity to Christ during the persecutions. As for the development of the Latin Church, Drure was inclined to broaden the religious and missionary presence and end the historic partition which divided the territory of the delegation between the Carmelites (south-central), Dominicans (north), and Capuchins (Upper Mesopotamia and Armenia Minor). Drure also wanted to establish a community of French Carmelite nuns in Baghdad, but Rome was not of the same opinion; they preferred that he expand the scope of the Dominican Sisters of the Presentation, who were soon given authorization to provide nursing care in the civil hospital of Baghdad. In Mosul, Drure thought of opening a novitiate for the Dominican Third Order, though his attempt to get the Salesians of Don Bosco to settle in the city, in order to establish and direct schools, proved in vain.

Meanwhile, the Dominican Berré—a zealous and exemplary religious—planned the opening of the Pie Maestre Indigene school, which was a great development in Europe at that time. In the same period (1911), the Congregation of the Sisters Chaldean Daughters of the Sacred Heart of Jesus was founded in Amadia for the education of illiterate girls, giving catechetical assistance in parishes, caring for the elderly, and supporting

---

Thomas, prot. no. 26384, dated September 9, 1909, in NA deposit Iraq in ASV.

abandoned youths.[129] In those same years, together with better formation for the clergy[130] and religious, a great effort was made toward the Christian education of children; it was clear that ignorance represented one of the worst evils the Church faced.

In the spring of 1907, Drure went to Rome for his *ad limina* visit and to deal with issues relating to his diocese and the apostolic delegation. He returned to Mesopotamia in 1912 as the political and religious situation in the Middle East was in upheaval: France (which had broken off relations with the Holy See and called into question the centuries of protection they had extended to Ottoman Catholics), Great Britain, Germany, and Italy all were trying to supplant each other and extend their own influence. Constantinople, in turn, opened an official representative office at the Vatican, further diminishing the role traditionally exercised by the protectorates. At the same time, nationalist unrest in the Balkans would soon lead to the Ottomans losing much of their European territory and foreshadowed difficult times to come for the Christian communities of Upper Mesopotamia. In this unfolding situation, the Holy See began to consider changes to the ecclesiastical territories. The first to propose a restructuring of their missions were the Capuchins, who, in 1909, through their superior general, asked Rome to change the Capuchin mission in Mesopotamia, passing the residences of Malatia, Karput, and Mamuret-ul-Aziz to the Capuchin mission in Syria, while continuing to depend on the Capuchin province of Lyon for their support; the rest of the mission would remain within the jurisdiction of the delegation of Mesopotamia and be taken

129. The initiative for the founding came from a pious priest named Ablahad Raes. In 1961 the sisters were forced to leave the villages where they served because of the war between the Kurds and the Baghdad government. On January 6, 1998, Patriarch Rafael Bidawid recognized the community as a patriarchal congregation.

130. Those were the years of *Haerent anima,* when Pius X, on the fiftieth anniversary of his ordination to the priesthood, exhorted the clergy of the whole world to pursue a life of real holiness.

over by the Capuchin province of Palermo. The Dominicans, however, proposed no changes, because their mission was fairly compacted around Mosul, which, at that time, was first under the guidance of Fr. Galland and then Fr. Berré, who, from 1922 would become the new apostolic delegate of Mesopotamia. Drure saw the beginning of the political changes and the demographic shifts which affected the Christians, but not their conclusion. He died on May 20, 1917, in France, where he had retired.

Chapter 4

The Twentieth Century

Demographic and Geographic Upheaval
and the Birth of Iraq

1. The Great Christian Demographic Crisis, and the Renewed Concern of the Holy for Eastern Catholics

As the twentieth century dawned, all the signs pointed toward a gathering storm. Popes Pius X (1903–14) and Benedict XV (1914–22) witnessed great changes that would transform both the Christian demography of Upper Mesopotamia and the geography of the Middle East. The Ottoman Empire, pulled apart from within by the various nationalities under Turkish oppression, was close to disintegration; ethnic and tribal strife within and world war without were about to reshape the profile of the whole region. The Christian community would be marked deeply by the experience of the coming years and would pay a heavy price in suffering, injustice, and violence. Secular France, under Prime Minister Emile Combes, renounced the concordat with the Holy See and suspended diplomatic relations, divorcing the nation from its faith. While this enabled the Church to appoint bishops in France free of civil interference, it left the Christians of the Ottoman Empire without their most powerful guardian. While Christians had, technically, been civilly emancipated since 1856 and the Crimean War, and were legally no different

119

than Muslims, this was a mere formality; anti-Christian purges and pogroms were an all too common. This was the case with the martyrs of Damascus, eight Franciscans and three Maronites, who were slaughtered during the Druze uprising of 1860; and with the Armenians, who came in for heavy persecution first under Sultan Abdul-Hamid II—who authorized paramilitary groups of Kurdish irregular soldiers to massacre the Armenian population, killing hundreds of thousands between 1894 and 1896—and then by the so-called Young Turks in 1909, who claimed the Armenians had aided Russia in its wars against the Ottomans. Between 1915 and 1918, a true genocide was organized and enacted: hundreds of thousands of Armenians were cruelly massacred, often with the complicity of the Kurds, or died of hunger and exhaustion either during their forced deportation or as they fled for their lives. Along with the Armenians, tens of thousands of Chaldeans and Christians of other confessions were also killed by the Turkish government.[1] Many of the survivors of the genocide would be expelled from their lands, together with the Christian missions, at the birth of the Turkish secular republic in 1921, and would disappear completely. Five bishops were martyred, and three more died in exile. Of the sixteen dioceses that had been established, only three remained active; out of 250 priests, about 126 were killed, along with several religious. In the summer of 1915, seven Catherinette nuns—an order founded only thirty-five years earlier—were slaughtered,

1. Congregation for the Eastern Churches, *Atti del Convegno di storia ecclesiastica contemporanea (Città del Vaticano, 22–24 ottobre 1998), La Questione armena: la Chiesa martire, in Fede e Martirio – Le Chiese orientali cattoliche nell'Europa del Novecento* (Vatican City: Libreria Editrice Vaticana, 2003); according to B. L. Zekeyan, "more than a million were physically exterminated during the chaos of World War I" (ibid., 164). M. Impagliazzo, *Una finestra sul massacro—Documenti inediti sulla strage degli armeni (1915–1916)* (Milan: Guerini e Associati, 2004). R. Roberson, *The Eastern Christian Churches* (Rome: Orientalia Christiana, 1999), 147. J. Yacoub, *Qui, s'en souviendra? 1915: le génocide assyro-chaldéo-syriaque* (Paris: Cerf, 2014).

including two founders of the congregation. A terrifying wave of blood, violence, and injustice swept across the region. In a contemporary report, the Dominican Father François Dominique Berré—then the superior at Mardin, and who witnessed at first hand the Turkish massacre of the Christians of that city—reported that they believed they came, "to liberate Turkey from its internal enemies, who are the Christians." The Turks were of the opinion that, as with the massacres of 1894–96, the European powers would not intervene to avenge their deaths; saying to themselves: "After all, our allies, the Germans, are there to support us."[2] Berré's report speaks of the death of thousands of men, women, and children, with obvious lies and invented accusations used as a pretext for their elimination. This was the case for the congregation of St. Francis of Assisi. It was denounced to the police as a French association, which was considered proof of treason against the Catholics of Mardin, who were all declared to be members of a French secret society.[3] The Dominican mission in Mosul was greatly tested by war; some of its buildings were demolished, and the rest were looted. In an appeal to the leaders of the warring peoples, on August 1, 1917, Benedict XV once again urged an end to war, but also invited consideration of real and practical proposals to establish "a just and lasting peace," as well as a settlement of equity and justice for the territories of the former Ottoman empire and "especially for Armenia."[4]

In the devastating fury of those terrible years, the apostolic delegate of Persia, Jacque-Emile Sontag, lost his life. He was killed in July of 1918, in the Vincentian mission in Urmia, together with the Chaldean archbishop of the city, Thomas Audo, and a large number of Christians. In Salmas, two Vincentians, a Chaldean priest, together with all the Christians, men, women,

2. *Rapport du T. R. P. Berré—Massacres de Mardin*, January 15, 1919, 2, in NA deposit Iraq in ASV.
3. Ibid., 16.
4. Benedict XV, *Ai capi dei popoli belligeranti* (*AAS* 9 [1917], 421–23).

children, were killed—all except the young women and girls, who had already been taken as plunder by the Persian lords. Turks, Persians, and Kurds all raged against the defenseless people, as was noted by Chaldean Bishop Aziz, who managed to escape the massacre.[5]

In consideration of this ongoing tragedy, the Apostolic See, which, under Pope Leo XIII, had already separated within Propaganda Fide its work *pro Orientalibus* from that *pro Infidelibus*, wanted to make an even stronger statement of solidarity with, and support for, the Eastern Churches. Benedict XV created the Sacred Congregation for the Eastern Churches in 1917, placing it outside of the supervision of Propaganda Fide and under his personal direction.[6] The new department was competent to handle all affairs relating to people, discipline, and rite for any of the Eastern Churches, including mixed cases in which any of the people concerned were of the Latin rite. In addition to this, and as signs of Christian solidarity, Benedict XV instituted the octave of prayer for Christian unity, proclaimed St. Ephrem a Doctor of the Church, and founded the Pontifical Institute for Oriental Studies, with the task of conducting preparatory work for the understanding of the East in the West.

2. The Hashemite Kingdom, the Republic, and Crisis and Development of the Church in Iraq

Upon the dissolution of the Ottoman Empire in 1915, Mesopotamia (modern Iraq) was divided into three *vilayets*, or prov-

---

5. A. Smets, *Memoire sur les massacres survenus dans les dioceses de Salmas et d'Ourmia*, in NA deposit Iraq in ASV.

6. Benedict XV, motu proprio *Dei providentis*, May 1, 1917; the pope himself served as prefect of the congregation, and he was assisted by a cardinal who acted as secretary (*AAS* 9 [1917], 529–31). Four popes would hold the office of prefect of the congregation: Benedict XV (1917–22), Pius XI (1922–39), Pius XII (1939–58), and John XXIII (1958–63).

inces: Baghdad, Basra, and Mosul. Turkey renounced its sovereignty of the middle, eastern territories, and a number of new nation-states were born. There were local governments with their national authorities and hierarchies, but these were influenced by the leaders of the most significant tribal or religious groups, which had exercised local authority within the empire and enjoyed a large degree of autonomy. On May 16, 1916, Britain and France struck the Sykes-Picot agreement over the division of the Ottoman provinces. Basra and Baghdad had been occupied by the British since 1914 and 1917 respectively, and would be brought under the British sphere of influence. Mosul and Kurdistan, together with Syria, were placed under French oversight. Kirkuk, with its oil reserves, continued under the administration of London. Despite that agreement, all of Mesopotamia from Basra to Mosul soon fell under British control, though not without protest from the French. In the formal division of the Middle East, conducted at San Remo in April of 1920, the French received Syria and Lebanon, and the British were given Palestine and Transjordan and formally ceded control of all of Mesopotamia. The French repeated their protests, and the disposition of Mosul and the northern border was deferred and changed again with the Treaty of Sèvres (August 10, 1920). The final geopolitical arrangement was resolved, following the Turkish-British dispute, with the decision of December 16, 1925, by the Council of the League of Nations.

With the emergence of Iraq as a political and territorial entity (1920) there followed a period of internecine strife and competing claims, which was a perennial constant in the history of this country. The religious geography (Shi'ites, Sunnis, Kurds) and traditional tribal zones of influence, and the factionalism of the multiplicity of "nations" in the area (Chaldeans, Assyrians, Syrians, Turkmen, Jews, Mandaeans, Yazidis, Shabak, Kaki) prevented a popular movement toward any lasting common unity. Indeed, the most significant ethnic and religious entities became increasingly closed, refractory, and distrustful of each other, trying to live apart within their historical-religious spheres, whose interests they pursued whenever they could, often inflaming tensions in the process. The Christian communities were also divided within this new nation and did not agree with each other. Instead, they were left to seek protection, either internationally or from the strongest local force available. The failure of the territorial claims made by the Chaldeans, Syriacs, and Armenians (with the exception of the Assyrians in the 1930s) left the Christian population, as always, tied to their villages and scattered over a vast territory; the forces of foreign or internal migration, and the pursuit of economic betterment, further dispersed them any- and everywhere they would be able to work to achieve a better standard of living.

The period of civil unrest began almost at once: in July 1920, in the lower and middle Euphrates region (Najaf and Karbala), there were struggles between Shi'ites who were either for or against the British;[7] and in the north, the Kurds harbored continuous resentment, feeling they had been betrayed in their expectations of an independent Kurdistan. Meanwhile, the Christians, decimated by the atrocious Turkish persecutions, found themselves without protectors and facing serious questions about their very survival. It was in this context, and with some considerable reservations, particularly among Sunnis, that there arose a growing movement for a truly independent Iraq and in favor of a nationalism which hitherto had been absent politically and which had promoted all the ideals the new country lacked: unity for the country, overcoming tribalism, overcoming religious and ethnic sectarianism, self-governance for the nation,

7. See M. Galletti, *Iraq, il cuore del mondo* (Rome: Edizioni Labrys, 2011), 50: "The larger cities remained firmly under British military control which, in October (1920), crushed the revolt. Six thousand Iraqis were killed, along with five hundred British and Indian soldiers."

and home management of national wealth and resources. The British protectorate viewed this nascent nationalism with suspicion, placing more faith in the established mechanisms of governance offered by the tribes and the city-provinces. This was reflected in the proposed Iraqi Constitution of 1925, which contained two legal codes, one for the tribes and the other for the cities. Within the British geopolitical sphere of the Middle East, Iraq was now a Hashemite monarchy, headed by the emir, Faysal I, as a constitutional monarch and with a representative and democratic government. According to the constitution, the king had the power to appoint and dismiss ministers, convene the bicameral parliament, and call elections. In truth, the monarchy needed British support to ensure its survival against the rising tide of nationalism. Uprisings were sometimes bloody, and Britain was not above the use of toxic gas, in some cases, for control of territory; they made a sad example of some villages around Kirkuk and Kurdistan.

The Kingdom of Iraq, in truth, had no basis in any historic geopolitical reality, nor was it inhabited by a single people;[8] it was a political creation of the victorious powers and a collapsed empire for a territory in which different nationalities, tribes, religions, and cultures had cohabited for centuries—the only borders they knew were the uncertain line of the desert on one side, and the Persian mountains on the other. The emir was po-

8. See U. Dann, *Iraq under Qassem: A Political History, 1958–1963* (Jerusalem: Israel Universities Press, 1969). The heterogeneity of Sunni Arabs, Shiites, Kurds, Turkmen, Christians, Jews, Yazidis, Sabeans, and Iranians had a decisive effect on Iraq's political life during the Ottoman period: the government was a fiction for a large part of it; the border with Persia was fluctuating, there was no regional or administrative infrastructure, as currently conceived, and orders rarely went beyond the boundaries of major cities. It was only with the imposition of European ideas that a real administrative system began to take shape; but twelve years of British mandate during Faisal's reign, who was himself a foreigner, did little to nurture loyalty to the idea of an Iraqi nation.

sitioned as a symbol of national identity to build around, and it was he who would ensure the unity of its people, assisted by a parliament and a government more inspired by European structures than the Arab tradition. This led to the constant confusion of roles and, eventually, to the military autocracy that would come to control Iraq and try to give cohesion to the country, despite ongoing discontent and riots. The Kurds, sacrificed by international politics, remained divided between Iraq, Turkey, Syria, and Iran, and became a source of often fierce resistance and instability for many years. Passing from Turkish domination to British oversight, Iraq became a country tightly controlled by Great Britain, which, in 1924, imposed upon a reluctant parliamentary assembly a treaty permanently establishing its military bases in the country, and giving Britain the right of veto on national legislation. It was during these politically troubled years that there was an increase in the middle class and a growing sympathy for pan-Arabism. Meanwhile, the economic structure of the country—which had always been mostly agricultural and mercantile—saw the first phases of real development, following the discovery of large oil deposits and the granting of the first exploration rights (1925).

On October 3, 1932, Iraq joined the League of Nations. In the twenty-five years between 1932 and 1958, the first royal succession took place, with the accession of Prince Ghazi in 1933. He was followed by his son Faisal II, in 1939. Faisal was still very young when he came to the throne, and he was placed under the regency of his uncle Abdul al'Ilah. The political scene at the time was dominated by instability, rivalries, and tensions. The 1933 massacre of Assyrian Christians, at the hands of the Kurdish general Sidqui Bakr al-Askari, led, in 1936, to the first of several military actions that would carry the pro-Axis Rashid Ali al-Gaylani to power in 1941; he was deposed by British intervention, which kept Iraq under occupation for the duration of

World War II and brought Abdul al'Ilah to power as a pro-British regent for the young King Faisal II. Postwar Iraq was strongly tied to the Palestinian cause and, in 1948, joined the Arab League. Nuri al-Saïd (1888–1958), a London man and influential politician who served as Iraqi prime minister eight times, dissolved parliament in 1954 and launched programs for industrial and agricultural development using the new revenue stream of oil royalties. To counter the influence of the USSR, who supported Kurdish nationalism, he orchestrated the Baghdad Pact of 1955 which tied Mesopotamia to the West; but his star declined rapidly with the rise of General Abd al-Karim Kassel, who, on July 14, 1958, launched a coup. Following its success, Kassel tore up the Baghdad Pact, executed Prime Minister al-Saïd and the entire royal family, and proclaimed Iraq to be a republic, opening a new chapter in the short and turbulent history of the fledgling nation.

With the fall of the Ottoman Empire, the ancient apostolic delegation of Mesopotamia, Kurdistan, and Armenia Minor found itself divided between the various new states. The Apostolic See, in view of these events, had not appointed a successor for François Drure following his departure for France. Instead, in October of 1919, an apostolic visitor was sent in the form of Bishop Adriaan Smets (1919–21), a canon of the Holy Sepulcher. He was supposed to take possession of the buildings of both the delegation and of St. John Seminary—which had been used as hospitals, first by the Turks and then by the British—but he delayed return of the buildings and the reopening of the seminary as an institute of training. Smets's immediate priority was to resume relations with the local Churches, which had been radically changed by the experience of persecution and war. He also moved to reorganize the Dominican mission, accepting the plan of their superior to start a vocational school and expand secondary education, and to refresh their pastoral initiatives in response to new demands. At the special instruction of Benedict XV, the new apostolic visitor took a special interest in the needs of war orphans, and was given large sums of money for their care.[9] Given the large number of boys, Smets initially divided them between the orphanages run by the Dominicans of Mosul and the Baghdad Carmelites, while studying the feasibility of creating a new institute within the headquarters of the delegation or of placing the children with good families. In the end, he decided upon the first option and wrote to the Congregation Pro Ecclesia Orientali (April 20, 1920); he believed that the creation of a new educational institution would be more in line with the wishes of the pope, education providing not only for the children's present circumstances but for their future as well. Meanwhile, he obtained the restitution of the property of both the delegation and the seminary, which was essential for their restoration, and reopened the seminary, with courses beginning in 1923. For the next ten years, the pupils were accommodated in the Chaldean seminary and the Syrian monastery of Mar Behnam. The reopening took place while the new Iraqi kingdom was still trying to organize its own education system; once this was in place, state interference would become a common problem. The British, meanwhile, as the new guardians of the region, were pushing for the old educational system to be replaced with something more efficient and entirely under government control.

Smets actively engaged with the situation of the Churches of Mesopotamia and did not fail to identify their particular

9. During the war, the Vatican created an important information office for prisoners, refugees, deportees, and for the impoverished civilian population of the occupied territories. Benedict XV wanted this work of solidarity to continue even after the war to help heal the terrible damage that had been caused, and to contribute to the reconciliation of the peoples; the papal support for war orphans and the people of Mesopotamia should be seen in this context.

problems.[10] He visited the dioceses of Zakho and Amadiya—then emerging from a five-year period of turmoil—and there he found much poverty, little education, and the places of worship in a deplorable state: "You could say stables, rather than churches," he remarked bitterly.[11] The problem, he noted, was not just the poverty of the people and the carelessness of those in charge, but also the lack of security "that you have in the land of the Kurds" and exorbitant taxes imposed by local chiefs. It was to alleviate these difficulties that, in 1922, the Opera di Assistenza a favore dei Profughi (later renamed the Catholic Near East Welfare Association, or CNEWA) was founded in the United States under papal auspices. It would provide incalculable support to the Churches and missionaries of the Congregation for the Eastern Churches.

Another group to suffer from the fallout of the collapse of the Ottomans were the Assyrian-Nestorians: the Assyrian "nation," about sixty thousand people, were led by the patriarch Shimon XIX Benjamin (1903–18) to abandon Qochanis, their traditional stronghold. His people dispersed, and the patriarch relocated to Urmia, where he was assassinated. He was succeeded by Shimon XX Paulos (1918–20) who moved the patriarchate to Mosul; he was soon succeeded by Shimon XXI Ishai (1920–75), who was twelve years old at the time (as the nephew of his predecessor, he came to office by hereditary suc-

10. In a document dated February 11, 1920, he identified them as: ignorance among the married clergy (who were living in the most remote villages, thus assuring a pastoral presence, but who did not instruct the faithful or reform their bad habits); rifts between the celibate, better-educated clergy and the married; economic abandonment of dioceses and parishes; a pervasive tribal and populist mentality; open criticism of religious leaders; shortage of canon law, and lack of respect for what little there was; and lack of spiritual initiatives in support of the religious life.

11. Following the destruction of the diocese of Gezira, Zakho had been entrusted with the spiritual care of nine additional Christian villages, added to the fifteen that already made up district; Amadiya had twenty Christian villages.

cession), and who quickly left to study in Britain, in Anglican schools. He returned to Iraq in 1929 only to be expelled in 1933. He found asylum first in Cyprus and then permanently in the United States. The Assyrian-Nestorians, left defenseless by the patriarchy and under constant political and territorial pressure, became refugees, first in Bakuba, near Baghdad, and then in various villages. Several thousand chose to go to Urmia, then under the political leadership of Agha Petros; others relied on the Iraqi government, which struggled to find alternative solutions for them. The Holy See, which followed this delicate situation with close attention, worked through the Opera per la Conversione dei Nestoriani, which had kept open about fifty small village schools since before the war, to provide as best it could for the most urgent needs of the displaced. In 1921, in view of the changed circumstances, the Opera was restructured into the Pontifical Commission for the Conversion of the Nestorians, led by the Chaldean patriarch Yousuf VI Emmanuel Thomas and assisted by several bishops and the superior of the Dominican mission.

In late December 1921, Smets left Iraq for Persia, where he was appointed apostolic delegate. He was recognized for his talents and appreciated for all he had managed to achieve in Mesopotamia.

Benedict XV, who both foresaw the horrors of war and experienced the consequences, was succeeded by Pope Pius XI (1922–39) who, with wisdom, energy, and tenacity, touched all areas of church life, showing to the world the power of the spiritual and moral mission of the Holy See. The day after his election, December 23, 1922, with the encyclical *Ubi arcano*, he set out his pontifical agenda, summarized in the expression "Pax Christi in regno Christi." In the seventeen years of his pontificate he celebrated three jubilee years, introduced the feast of Christ the King into the liturgical calendar, increased the number of dioceses within the Church, and expanded the missions among the pagans. He attached great importance to the continued efforts for reunion with the Orthodox Churches, which, like his predecessors, he saw as a return of separated brethren to the Catholic Church. He oversaw relations with the Eastern Catholic Churches, increasing—with the motu proprio *Sancta Dei ecclesia* (March 25, 1938)—the powers of the Congregation Pro Ecclesia Orientali, to which he granted exclusive jurisdiction over the Near East (Egypt, Palestine, Transjordan, Cyprus, Turkey, Syria, Lebanon, Iraq, and Iran).[12] For the study and development of Eastern theology and liturgy, he supported the foundation of the Istina Institute in Paris and the Pontifical Russicum College in Rome. He also formed a commission for the preparation of a new Eastern code of canon law. Cardinal Tisserant, secretary of the Congregation for the Eastern Churches, spoke of him as a pontiff who "had continuously given the sharpest attention of his intellect and the very pulse of his hope and his love" to the Eastern rites of Christianity.[13]

While the world watched the gathering storm, Pius XI's eventual successor, Eugenio Cardinal Pacelli (Pope Pius XII, 1939–58), tried to use the moral authority of the Apostolic See to prevent the imminent Second World War. His work to ameliorate the material needs of civilians, prisoners, and exiles is beyond dispute. In the ecclesial field, he showed particular care for the Eastern Churches. Cardinal Tisserant, in a circular to all the employees of his department informing them that Pius XII had assumed the prefecture of the congregation, wrote that the East had in him "another pastor … lovingly attentive to our every need and every hope," as his knowledge of oriental issues was well known and "often handled by him with vigilant attention

12. *AAS* 30 (1938), 154–59.
13. Letter of Congregation for the Eastern Churches, no. 133/39, dated February 11, 1939, in NA deposit Iraq in ASV.

in his various offices." With the encyclical *Orientalis ecclesiae* (1944), the pope reaffirmed the principle that, in the event of reunion, no one would be forced to abandon their traditions and rituals,[14] and in the following year (1945), with the encyclical *Orientales omnes ecclesias*, he reminded everyone of the Union of Brest and the importance of that act;[15] finally, with *Orientales ecclesias* (1952), he denounced the oppression of the Eastern Catholics at the hands of the Soviet regime.[16] Pius XII also took charge of the updating of Eastern ecclesiastical law and, through various documents, provided for certain norms that remained in force until the publication of the Code of Canons of the Eastern Churches in 1990, including the reservation of matters of ritual transfer to the congregation; renewing the discipline of marriage law (*Crebrae allatae*, 1949); revising procedural law (*Sollicitudinem nostram*, 1950); reforming laws concerning the rights of religious and temporal goods (*Postquam apostolicis litteris*, 1952); and instituting new norms for different rites and the right of the faithful (*Cleri sanctitati*, 1957). It was Pius XII who laid the foundations for what would become the era of ecumenism with his important instruction of 1950 in which he spoke of the ecumenical movement as a work of the Holy Spirit.[17]

Against the backdrop of these thirty years (1920–50) of activity by the Roman pontiffs focusing on Eastern matters, we can examine the most significant events that touched the lives of the Christians of Mesopotamia. It must be said that, basi-

14. *ASS* 36 (1944), 129–47. On the occasion of the fifteenth centenary of the death of St. Cyril of Alexandria, the pope, recalling the saint's teachings and fidelity to the See of Peter, argued for the healthy application of his example to the present times.

15. *AAS* 38 (1946), 33–63. In the 350th anniversary of the union of the Ruthenian Church with the Catholic Church, Pius XII reminded the bishops of the world of the event and explained its significance, and its example of hope and encouragement for Catholics under persecution.

16. *AAS* 35 (1953), 524.

17. *De Motione oecumenica*, *AAS* 32 (1950), 142–51.

cally, those were peaceful years in which the Christians of that land had a chance to tend the wounds of the first two decades of the century. There were no real persecutions, at least on the scale that there had been, and the British-backed monarchy was, in fact, a good guarantor of fairness for the minority population of the kingdom. While ordinary Christians had no voice in the management of political and economic affairs, under the authority of the Chaldean patriarch bishops had the ability to speak on behalf of their communities, and the presence of the apostolic delegate favored a relaxed atmosphere that allowed Catholic families to take care of their own welfare, educate their children, and organize the development of their respective religious communities. The consolidation of the dioceses, redrawn to accommodate the new political geography, fueled the hope that local churches would still have a future.

In December 1921, shortly before his death, Benedict XV appointed the Dominican François Dominique Berré as the Latin archbishop of Baghdad. Soon afterward, on September 19, 1922, Pius XI also entrusted him with the office of apostolic delegate for Mesopotamia, Kurdistan, and Armenia Minor. As a missionary, he had arrived in Mosul in 1884 and had worked as a professor at St. John Seminary; and he went on to become the superior of the Dominican mission. During the war he had been imprisoned in Turkey for four years and then deported to France, where he continued to take an interest in the Dominican mission in Iraq. When the war ended, he returned to reestablish the mission, which he found almost completely destroyed. It fell to him to repair the buildings of the delegation and of the inter-ritual seminary, which had been occupied by the British and used as a hospital, and reopen it for study. He was also responsible for the successful reordering of the Opera per la Conversione dei Nestoriani and for running the Benedict XV orphanage—which Berré immediately took to his heart—

and which had been placed under the guardianship of the apostolic delegation. Providing for the orphans was his first priority, and he continued the work begun by Smets as apostolic visitor. He cared greatly for the boys who lived at the residence, and they had a great affection for him for, as he himself pointed out, these were boys who came from not just from the streets of Mosul, but from Urmia, Seert, and Mardin. They were often abandoned, dependent upon begging, homeless, and without anyone to deal with them, except the police. Some of the boys had been bought by Muslims or the Kurds, who used them as slaves, and, not infrequently, they were the children of martyrs and confessors of the faith. The orphanage became home to sixty boys, who lived there thanks to the help of both private benefactors and the delegation itself, which provided their education and vocational training. After his transfer of the delegation to Baghdad, Berré entrusted the orphanage to the Dominicans, who assumed its spiritual, disciplinary, and administrative direction, leaving the apostolic delegate with supervisory control, similar to that which he exercised toward the other pious works of the Dominicans in the territory.

The social work of the Church, especially toward children, had become an indispensable support for the Christian community following what they had come to call the "great tribulation": the population lived in terrible circumstances, many Christian villages had been destroyed, the displaced were living in makeshift accommodations, the future was uncertain. Many of them felt a sense of betrayal by international organizations, which offered little protection as they endured systematic injustice from the courts and struggled to secure themselves against the murder and plunder to which they were still frequently subjected. Notwithstanding the law of 1922,[18] the administration of justice in the new kingdom of Iraq had not changed; the Qur'an

18. The Anglo-Iraqi treaty of October 10 granted universal freedom of

remained the only valid law, and the testimony of Muslims had preeminence over that of "infidels" be they Christian or of other religions. Christian villages were punitively taxed, and then systematically ignored by the administration, left without medical services, drinking water, or irrigation. A report edited by the Commission of the Council of the League of Nations, dated July 16, 1925, spoke specifically of the Mosul region as a territory in which "protective measures must be taken on behalf of minorities and the restoration of ancient rights and practices before the war" and insisted that "all Christians be ensured religious freedom and the right to open schools."[19]

Berré, well aware of the situation after his long years in the Dominican mission, did not spare Rome the details, transmitting in-depth reports from the missions and dioceses. In a letter dated December 15, 1924, one Fr. Basile, a Capuchin from Mamouret ul-Aziz (Turkey), described the condition of the Mardin mission: "Of our six more or less compromised or destroyed stations, it only, Mézéré, that is, the college, the church, and the girls' school, which survived the destructive action of the hordes who passed by there.... Three nearby villages no longer have one stone upon another between them; but the [missionary] station of Orfa has been reoccupied by the fathers returned from France and Malatia [Melitene], they have been able to retain the presence of the Armenian Catholic bishop, despite the authorities who wish to oust him, since he lived there alone with thirty Christian families; emigration has been relentless, and the Christians reduced to a handful."[20] In January of 1926 more violence afflicted the villages of Azekh, Mediat, Ain-Warde, Enhel, Mezizakh and Djebel-Tour,

conscience, and the constitution of the kingdom was obliged to comply with this provision.

19. Archive of Berré, document of the Commission of the Council of the League of Nations, in NA deposit Iraq in ASV.

20. Archive of Berré, letter dated December 15, 1924, in NA deposit Iraq in ASV.

raising the protests of the Apostolic See to the Turkish authorities. On December 28 of the same year, the Catholics of Marga (the Kurdish region northeast of Mosul, including the villages of Matha, Bechalla, Beyaldo and Bekika) were forcibly expelled to accommodate a new border demarcation.[21] As apostolic delegate, Berré begged Rome to send him economic aid to alleviate the plight of the refugees, and he was given generous support by Pius XI.[22] Turkish harassment and arrests of many Christians, and some members of the Jacobite clergy, continued in Djebel and Azekh, as punishment for having returned to communion with the pope, who had defended them through his apostolic delegate in Constantinople.

At a 1927 papal audience granted to Berré, Pius XI emphasized to his delegate the pastoral care of the Yazidis, the spiritual care of the clergy, the collaboration between Chaldeans and Syrians, and special attention to schools. The pope specifically wished to see the establishment in Iraq of an institute of higher learning, and, on July 7, 1928, the pope approved its creation and guaranteed a reasonable annual subsidy for its maintenance; but he wanted it to be a clearly Catholic institution and run by English-speaking religious.[23] As ordinary of the Latins, Berré produced some significant pastoral writings, such as the letter on "Brotherly Love as the Distinguishing Mark of Christians" (Lent 1926), and the "Nature of the Church as Founded on

21. Archive of Berré, report dated January 4, 1925; report no. 232 of December 28, 1926, in NA deposit Iraq in ASV.
22. Archive of Berré, letter of thanks from the clergy and the faithful, in NA deposit Iraq in ASV.
23. Archive of Berré, letter no. 276/28, dated August 31, 1928, in NA deposit Iraq in ASV. Patriarch Yousuf VI Emmanuel Thomas had, for some time, been trying to open a college in Baghdad, and had even earmarked a sum of twenty thousand rupees for the project; in addition to its educational work, the college also maintained two Chaldean orphanages, one for girls and one for boys (archive of Berré, letter to Cardinal Marini, dated July 1, 1922, 61–74, in NA deposit Iraq in ASV).

Christ, Professing the Same Faith, and United Under One Shepherd" (Lent 1927). His teaching often made it across to the other local Churches, with whom he maintained good relations. During his tenure, Patriarch Yousuf VI Emmanuel Thomas founded the congregation of the Chaldean Daughters of Mary Immaculate (1922) in Baghdad, for the education of poor and abandoned youth and the teaching of catechism, and for works of charity and the support of parishes.[24] The first group of six religious was soon part of a rapidly expanding community. In the same period, on April 4, 1928, the pope approved the Congregation of the Third Order of Indigenous Governesses also called the Indigenous Tertiary of St. Catherine of Siena, which was set up to provide for the education of poor girls and the care of the sick and needy.[25] The two congregations were intended to respond to the growing needs of the Church in Iraq at the time, and to the powerful attraction to the religious life which many young people feel at all times and in all places. Berré had, in fact, always been in favor of the founding of indigenous religious communities, considering them better suited to respond to the mentality and needs of the local population. He also complained that young people from poorer backgrounds were not always welcomed by the Western congregations, if not considered outright as second-class applicants; Berré saw, therefore, that it was a waste to send aspirants to European convents, where they of-

24. On May 20, 1923, Patriarch Yousuf VI Emmanuel Thomas notified the Congregation for the Eastern Churches that the priests Antonio Zibouni and Philippe Shauriz, following the encouragement of the same patriarch, had given birth to a new community of women with ten girls, gathered in a house; and they had started their novitiate year on Assumption Day; the patriarch was confident that this new congregation would be devoted to the various needs of his Church (archive of Berré, letter no. 10509/23 of August 10, 1923, in NA deposit Iraq in ASV). The congregation was erected on August 7, 1922.

25. In 1935 the constitutions received final approval, and the apostolic delegate became the ordinary; religious were asked to keep to the rite in which they were baptized.

ten found it very hard to adjust. He preferred, instead, that they were placed under the direction of the Latin missionaries, while maintaining the link with their own particular ritual Churches: "Latin missionaries will have at heart the intention to inspire their attachment to their own rites and submission to their spiritual leaders."[26]

In April 1929 Berré died at Mosul and his work was entrusted to his secretary, the Dominican Antonin Drapier, who had served as a missionary in Mosul.[27] On October 7, 1929, he was elected titular archbishop of Neocaesarea Pontus and appointed apostolic delegate for Mesopotamia, Kurdistan, and Armenia Minor; on November 26 he also became apostolic administrator of Baghdad of the Latins, as well as continuing on as the apostolic delegate. He held these posts until November 19, 1936, when he was transferred to the apostolic delegation in Indochina.

While the majority of Mesopotamia had been gathered in the kingdom of Iraq, the Delegation continued to have within its purview territory that was now a part of other states, including Turkey and Syria. The political changes, the persecutions, and the exodus of many Christians profoundly changed the geography of dioceses. The resulting review of their territories took place at the end of Drapier's time in office, and he was in favor of transferring Upper Gezira to the apostolic delegation for Syria, being now within the borders of that country. In addition, it was decided to transfer the headquarters of the delegation from Mosul to Baghdad, the capital of the kingdom; this was done in the spring of 1936.

Drapier's time in office was marked by many important political events: the admission of the Kingdom of Iraq to the League of

26. Archive of Berré, collection of minutes: *Notice sur la formation des Communautés de Religieuses indigènes dans les Missions d'Orient*, 5–21, Rome, June 3, 1919, in NA deposit Iraq in ASV.

27. He was born at Creuse-en-Woevre, in the diocese of Verdun, on April 28, 1891.

Nations (1932), which had intervened in 1925 to resolve a conflict with Turkey concerning the province of Mosul; the annulment of the twenty-five year treaty of alliance imposed by Great Britain; and the end of the insurrection of the small Assyrian-Nestorian communities (1933), which was crushed by the military government, resulting in the loss of many lives.[28] The crushing of the Assyrian-Nestorian revolt was used by Baghdad to create a precedent and discourage any future minority uprisings, and Patriarch Shimon XXI Ishai, stripped of his Iraqi citizenship, was forced into exile in the United States. Against this backdrop, Drapier was instructed to maintain good relations with the king, assuring him that Catholics would not press any territorial claims for autonomy, and would support the national identity and unity of the country; in return, he only demanded a guarantee of their religious rights, which were not in opposition to the unity of the young kingdom. Faced with the temptation to join in and support of the claims of the Assyrian-Nestorians and to form an independent state or autonomous region, Iraq's Catholics were supposed to show up and be good citizens and to cooperate in the prosperity of the country, in line with the decision of the local Catholic hierarchy.

In ecclesial affairs, the first priority was to promote meetings of the Iraqi episcopate, without distinction of rite, in *amicabiles conventus*, to discuss the most suitable means of ensuring the progress of Catholicism in the country. In this important project the delegate had the approval and encouragement of the Apostolic See, and he worked to convince the local bishops of the opportunities these meetings presented. To help illustrate the possibilities of better cooperation, in the spring of 1931 he set an ambitious agenda that included education, the commemoration of the Council of Ephesus, the foundation of Catholic Action,

28. Several hundred people were killed in the suppression of the revolt, including several Catholic priests.

the unification of the ecclesiastical courts, and other significant projects.

One major event in the history of the Iraqi Church at that time was the arrival of the Jesuits in Baghdad.[29] Their presence was in response to a request from the Iraqi hierarchy, who wished to implement the pope's desire for an Iraqi school of higher education to provide both personal and educational formation for Catholic children. Rome had asked the Jesuits of Boston to lead the project, and they obtained permission to open the Baghdad College from the Iraqi Ministry of Education on June 30, 1932. Construction began in 1936 on a large building that would house a thousand boys. In the five years of study, the students would be educated in preparation for a bachelor of arts degree in civil engineering and administration sciences, which would open the doors of American universities. It was an institution of great cultural and religious importance, and was frequented by Muslims and Christians, almost in equal numbers, as well as some Jewish students. It would form a large part of the Iraqi intellectual and professional classes. Meanwhile, Drapier, together with the local religious authorities, took charge of the Syrian school being erected in Mosul, and worked for the protection of minorities in Iraq[30] and the reconstitution of pastoral life in Upper Mesopotamia.[31] Another important issue was the defense of St. John Semi-

29. In 1931 the Iraqi-American Educational Association was founded and recognized by the U.S. government, and the Iraqi Ministry of Education granted them permission to open a school. The first four Jesuits arrived in Baghdad in 1932 and started the Baghdad College on Muraba Street; two years later they settled in the Sulaikh district; from 1934 to 1969 (the year of confiscation) seventy religious worked there, also engaging with Al-Hikmah University, which opened in 1956.

30. According to statistical data of 1935 (Jewish Agency for Palestine, Economic Research Institute, *Statistical Handbook of Middle Eastern Countries* [Jerusalem: D. B. Aaronson, 1945]), Iraq was home to an estimated 110,885 Christians of various rites, of which 78,355 lived in the northern provinces and 31,671 in the south-central provinces.

31. Repeated requests had been raised by the missionaries at this time,

nary against the attempts of the civil authorities not to exempt pupils from service "to the flag," and to equate the religious institution with an ordinary state secondary school and take control, even though the seminary was designated as a "religious school." The Chaldean patriarch Yousuf VI Emmanuel Thomas had to defend the right to manage his own seminary, which he considered "the joy of the (Chaldean) nation," whose seminarians animated the liturgical life of his cathedral, which saw "beautiful and ancient ceremonies that touch the hearts of the people and bring them to church to hear their shepherd's voice"; and he added, also "our separated brethren envy us, seeing that it (the seminary) preserves with us the antiquity of our ritual, which they have lost."

In the spring of 1936, orders came from Rome instructing Drapier to leave Mosul and to transfer the headquarters of the delegation to Baghdad. In truth, he had been *persona non grata* in Iraq for some time, and he was accused of being too close to the French consul in Mosul. This was why, following anti-Christian turmoil in 1935, his name had surfaced in a trial involving some Christians. The Iraqi diplomat in Italy, Muhazil al-Pachachi, had spoken to the Vatican, indicating that his country would, in the future, no longer accept an apostolic delegate from France, England, or Italy; they far preferred, instead, to have a representative from a less significant state, such as Belgium or the Netherlands. He had also asked that the delegation be moved to Baghdad, and that the jurisdiction of the delegate be limited to the Iraqi borders. Finally, he expressed, more out of courtesy than conviction, the hope of establishing diplomatic relations between the Holy See and Iraq. The idea was not new;

---

demanding the establishment of new parishes for the faithful who still resided in Upper Gezira, despite the tens of thousands of martyrs who had sacrificed their lives, the forced exiles, and the destruction of the dioceses. See archive of Drapier, letter no. 859/26, dated March 8, 1937: Monsignor Hindié to the Apostolic Delegation of Mesopotamia, in NA deposit in Iraq in ASV.

since the early 1930s, in fact, there had been some contact; and the Vatican had not shown itself to be against the idea, provided that the initiative came formally from the Iraqi government. The Holy See was particularly concerned with two points: the protection of the religious rights of minorities, particularly of Catholics, and the protection of the Catholic schools. But Britain, influential in the foreign policy of the Iraqi government, had signaled its reservations; and the project was shelved. The issue was noted, but the time was not ripe. Drapier, aware of the delicate situation in which he found himself, was clear that he was willing to leave Iraq if his presence was considered inappropriate; indeed, he came to see it as a necessity, and declared himself in favor of the appointment of a new delegate coming from a more neutral country. His transfer to Baghdad was felt as a real loss by the Catholics in Mosul, given his long and praiseworthy presence among the Christian communities of the Plain of Nineveh and Kurdistan. His departure marked the end of papal representation residing in that city. A few months later, he was transferred to Indochina, where by a lucky coincidence, he met Bishop Georges de Jonghe d'Ardoye, who, for health reasons, was leaving for Europe. Drapier predicted that he would be the best person to replace him in Iraq, not least because of his Belgian nationality.

At the time of Drapier's departure, there was little in the way of overt hostility to Christians, and the government guaranteed a relative freedom of worship. But, there were still difficulties with the government, especially concerning education; and there was a real lack of people capable of making a firm and effective defense of the Church and her rights. The Chaldean patriarch, Yousuf VI Emmanuel Thomas, had to surrender the governance of his own schools in Baghdad, Basra, and Mosul; and there was little likelihood of his regaining control. Within his Church, the faithful showed an intense piety, but there was little in the way of religious culture; the priests, despite having a good education themselves, omitted preaching and often lacked any deep spiritual formation. Meanwhile, pastoral activity was limited to the traditional observances and lacked any missionary impetus. Muslim conversions were unheard of, and what conversions there were came from among the Nestorians, especially in cases of mixed marriages.

With the transfer of the delegation to Baghdad, the Holy See took the opportunity to restructure its territorial remit, adapting it to the new geopolitical reality and changing its title to apostolic delegation to Iraq.[32]

3. Instability and War in Iraq: The Complex Role of the Church

As Europe suffered the ravages of the rise of Nazism and Fascism, the consequences were felt as far away as Iraq; the violent new ideologies found a welcome home in some corners of the Iraqi press and the ascent of Hitler's Germany was hailed as a welcome challenge to British dominance. Fascist ideology mixed easily with local agendas, with the Turks striving to keep alive old sympathies, the Kurds always looking to forge any consensus toward their independence, and Iraqi nationalism quickly morphing into xenophobia and the pan-Arabism that was gaining traction among the youth.

On September 5, 1939, the government of Iraq, under British pressure, broke off diplomatic relations with Germany; the military forces of Iraq—which included an army of twenty-five thousand soldiers and a small air force—were nothing compared to the importance of the Iraqi oil fields, whose terminals reached the Mediterranean and the Persian Gulf. In support of the war

32. *Decree of the Congregation for the Eastern Churches*, no. 120/29, dated September 24, 1938, and letter no. 120/29, dated November 14, 1938, in NA deposit Iraq in ASV.

effort, Baghdad granted every request to come out of London, and broke off diplomatic relations with the other Axis powers of Italy and Japan. The initially pro-German sentiment in the country was short-lived,[33] and Prime Minister Rashid Ali al-Gaylani was eventually forced to flee the country. A new government was formed on June 2, 1941, but the instability left an opening for disorder; and many of Baghdad's Jews saw their homes and their property looted, as did more than a few Christian families, with a church also being attacked. On November 16, 1941, Iraq's foreign minister broke off relations with the Vichy government of occupied France, and the French Embassy was closed. Then, on January 16, 1943, Iraq formally declared war on the Axis nations, though the war, properly speaking, never reached its borders. British military operations, from Persia to Palestine, kept Mesopotamia under tight control, especially along the Turkish front; and Iraq became little more than a space for military reserve operations, a place to park seventy thousand Polish soldiers, and a jail for Italian and German prisoners.[34]

With the insidious advance of National Socialism in Europe and around the world, Iraq's apostolic delegation had been instructed to be on guard; then Secretary of State Pacelli, in a private letter, urged the heads of mission to be on alert against the subversive methods of Nazi diplomacy as well, as Germany was becoming

33. The German embassy remained open for quite some time after the cessation of formal relations, and it actively sought to stoke anti-British sentiment.

34. See *Le Saint Siège et la guerre en Europe, Novembre 1942–Décembre 1943*, vol. 7 of *Actes et documents du Saint Siège relatifs à la Seconde Guerre Mondiale*, ed. P. Blet et al. (Vatican City: Libreria Editrice Vaticana, 1973), 436; Le Saint Siège et les victimes de la guerre, Janvier–Decembre 1943, vol. 9 of *Actes et documents du Saint Siège relatifs à la Seconde Guerre Mondiale*, ed. P. Blet et al. (Vatican City: Libreria Editrice Vaticana, 1975), 69.

the most serious persecutor of the Catholic Church [denounced by the encyclical *Mit brennender sorge*] and the [Nazi] authorities do not show any restraint in their attacks on ecclesiastical persons or affairs, their official printing continuously offends the dignitaries of the Church and the Holy Father through cartoons and articles … [while] the foreign diplomatic agents of the Third Reich show consideration toward the Church and its representatives, apparently in order to give the false impression that in Germany the Church is respected. Now the dignitaries of the Church must not let themselves be deluded if somewhere those representing Germany approach them with kindness … It is clear that the grave situation of the Church in Germany requires in all special papal representatives exercise of careful vigilance.[35]

When Pacelli became Pope Pius XII he would order that Vatican citizenship be awarded to all the staff of the various apostolic delegations (July 6, 1940) in order to preserve their formal neutrality and freedom to act, and ensure their safety during the time of global war.[36] At the same time, he reordered papal delegations and embassies, including that of Iraq, to act almost as humanitarian outreach agencies in favor of the civilian populations, prisoners, and exiles.

With the departure of Drapier, the delegation had been entrusted to the temporary care of the American Jesuit William Rice (1936–38), who was vicar general of the Latin archdiocese of Baghdad. Arranging a permanent successor was not easy. The Iraqi government strongly resisted the appointment of another Frenchman as apostolic delegate. Indeed, they hardly conceded the appropriateness of a foreign papal delegate in the country

---

35. Letter from the secretariate of state, prot. no. 3117/37, dated August 6, 1937, in NA deposit Iraq in ASV.

36. On this point, see Chapter 5, "Al tempo del trionfo del Reich," 125–54, in Fr. Blet's work *La Seconda Guerra Mondiale negli Archivi Vaticani*, Italian translation by Fr. E. P. Pacelli, ed. R. Di Castro (Rome: San Paolo, 1999).

at all and floated the idea that the office would be better held by an Iraqi archbishop, for example the Chaldean patriarch.[37] France, which resumed diplomatic relations with the Apostolic See in 1924, two decades after it severed all ties, intervened with the government in Baghdad to press home the need to respect the Geneva conventions on freedom of religion, including the freedom of the Church to govern itself autonomously (rather an ironic cause for France to champion, all things considered), and to remind the Iraqis of the moral force exerted internationally by the Apostolic See, which they would do well not to discount. It also reminded the government that the existence of the apostolic delegation predated the Iraqi kingdom, and, of course, that France historically had held an important role in the region. The Vatican and Paris even considered the possibility of entrusting the offices of the apostolic delegate and the Latin archbishopric to different people. Taking everything into account, the Holy See decided to appoint Rice as apostolic delegate, but without elevating him to the episcopal dignity. Iraq's representative to the Quirinale, Minister al-Pachachi, was informed of the decision *sub secreto*. He objected, first, that there had been no prior notice to or consent of the Iraqi government,[38] as, according to him, would have been extended as a courtesy to other governments; and second, that Rice, being a U.S. citizen, was the citizen of a powerful nation, something the Iraqi government had expressly opposed. The impasse forced Rome to stall for time, and Rice was told that the publication of his appointment had been held up by diplomatic complications.[39] In truth, the Vatican was not convinced that this was indeed the thought of the Iraqi govern-

37. The patriarch himself was no stranger to the idea, and his support was extensively courted by the government.

38. Letter to Fr. Rice from Cardinal Pacelli, prot. no. 1/116, dated February 9, 1938, in NA deposit Iraq in ASV.

39. Letter of the Congregation for Eastern Churches, prot. no. 99/37, dated June 3, 1937, in NA deposit Iraq in ASV.

ment; nor did it wish to break with the practice of not asking a government for permission to appoint apostolic delegates. Rice and the Chaldean patriarch brought the matter to the Iraqi authorities; but the thing dragged on, over the considerable objections of France, who wanted to restore the previous practice of appointing a Frenchman to the role. In June 1938, Rice was summoned to Rome, where the issue was to be resolved. It was then that the candidacy of the then bishop de Jonghe d'Ardoye began to take shape, and in October he was designated as the new apostolic delegate. Rice, rather disappointed by the whole affair, left Baghdad on January 20, 1939, to become the apostolic vicar of Belize.

Bishop Georges de Jonghe d'Ardoye belonged to a noble family; his father had been a senator of the kingdom of Belgium. He entered the Society for Foreign Missions in Paris, and had become a priest on May 21, 1910. A year later he began work as a missionary in China, where he distinguished himself for his work in education and youth, founding new schools and creating the Chinese Catholic Youth, which he directed until 1931.[40] On May 23, 1933, he was elected titular bishop of Amathous in Cyprus and appointed to the apostolic vicariate of Yünnanfu, where he remained until 1936, when, for health reasons, he had to return to Europe. It was following this that he received his appointments as titular archbishop of Mistia and apostolic delegate for Iraq. The new delegate arrived in Baghdad on November 12, 1938, took possession of his office, and met with Fr. Rice. A few days later, he was cordially received by the Iraqi foreign minister, Tawfiq al-Suwaidi, who expressed his satisfaction that the Holy See had accepted the government's requests that the delegation be moved to Baghdad and the appointment go to someone from a smaller country. The Holy See was, in turn,

40. The bishop was born on April 23, 1887, in Saint-Gilles-les Bruxelles, in the archdiocese of Malines.

satisfied that it had not departed from its own practice, and had appointed de Jonghe without asking prior consent from the Iraqi authorities. The dispute was considered to have been resolved amicably for all concerned, and, in a letter to King Ghazi I, Secretary of State Pacelli spoke of de Jonghe as a clergyman "eminent for his virtue and talent" and recommended him to the king's "supreme benevolence."[41]

Soon after, the new Iraqi government changed its attitude toward the apostolic delegate, viewing him with suspicion and, though he was esteemed by French diplomats, even considering him too anti-French because of his past in China, where he had several times defended the spirit of *Maximum illud* against interference by the colonial governments in matters of religion. With the international situation already tense enough, it was agreed to be patient and wait for better times. This was also the opinion of Tawfiq al-Suwaidi, who committed himself to pleading the delegate's cause and to help the new government understand his role; the crisis eventually resolved itself. In 1941 de Jonghe wrote to Rome that the papal presence had been established in Baghdad without serious incident. Being Belgian, under the terms of the papal bull *Super universas* of 1638, he could not be granted the see of the archdiocese of Baghdad of the Latins. This posed the question of whether or not to appoint an ordinary for the diocese who was not a bishop. The idea was supported by de Jonghe, who, in February 1939, wrote to Cardinal Tisserant in these terms: "This answer to the question of the archdiocese of Baghdad is the best and I well hope that which is temporary becomes permanent"; he added:

41. Letter to the king of December 24, 1938, in NA deposit Iraq in ASV. King Ghazi died on April 3, 1939, in a car accident; he was succeeded by his son Faisal II, a four-year-old, under the regency of Prince Abd al-Ilah. On the occasion of his coronation on April 25, 1953, Pius XII sent him his "warmest congratulations" and wishes "of prosperity," in the hope that "many long years of reign will bring peace and prosperity to the people of Iraq."

From the political point of view, the appointment of a French archbishop would be unfortunate, because the government of Iraq is always suspicious, they would be convinced that the appointment of a delegate of Belgian nationality would be nothing more than a camouflage, if appointed to his side is a French archbishop. The Minister (Plenipotentiary) of France seems resigned to having a French administrator, if not the archbishop he was expecting. If the administrator could remain superior of the Carmelite mission, this would be even better, because here we have enough religious leaders, and that is what is paralyzing all initiatives.[42]

Despite these well-reasoned reservations, Rome, under pressure from France, decided otherwise; and on April 1, 1939, appointed the Carmelite Armand M. Stéphane Blanquet du Chayla, as Latin archbishop of Baghdad.[43] De Jonghe d'Ardoye, no longer responsible for the administration of the Latin Church, remained in charge of St. John Seminary in Mosul and Benedict XV's orphanage. He also retained oversight of the Tertiary Dominican Sisters of St. Catherine of Siena, and he was able to give more attention to the Chaldean patriarchal seminary as well. Additionally he founded a Catholic primary school in the Karada neighborhood of Baghdad, intending it to become a modern educational institution responsive to the needs of a developing country; and he encouraged the Dominicans of Mosul to open a secondary college—the only establishment of its kind for the Christians of northern Iraq, and not unlike that which the Jesuits ran in Baghdad. De Jonghe d'Ardoye also showed particular concern for young people and encouraged the institution of the Catholic Youth of Baghdad, as he had done in the days when he was in China. He also wanted the Arabic language to become the first priority in the missionary schools and pleaded for the

42. Letter no. 112/90, dated February 19, 1939, in NA deposit Iraq in ASV.
43. Born at Brest, in the diocese of Quimper, on April 10, 1887, he entered the Carmelite Order and was ordained a priest on December 23, 1922.

establishment of an inspectorate for Catholic schools in Iraq. He was deeply concerned with the unity of Christians, which the Congregation for the Eastern Churches strongly encouraged;[44] he complained about certain attitudes and habits among the clergy, such as the fact that many did not preach in churches on Sunday; and he criticized the missionaries for not speaking Arabic, which seriously limited their apostolate. As a shepherd, he measured the suitability of the religious by their ability to evangelize, and he was not impressed: "I have not yet found the missionary spirit, the spirit of initiative, which dominated the Far East missions," he commented in a report in May 1940.[45] He strongly encouraged the ancient religious orders operating in Iraq to commit to reviving their presence and make a more generous commitment of manpower. He also wanted to see a serious improvement in the catechesis in Catholic schools, and he took the initiative to convene the clergy, including bishops and the Chaldean patriarch, leading them in spiritual meetings, and then publishing accounts of the conferences in the bulletin of St. John Seminary in Mosul.

44. Letter of the Congregation for the Eastern Churches, no. 701/38, dated November 14, 1939, in NA deposit Iraq in ASV. On November 11, 1939, Pius XII recommended to Cardinal Tisserant the Octave of Prayer for Christian Unity, which Benedict XV had inaugurated in 1916 and in which Pius XI, with the motu proprio *Ecclesia sancta Dei*, had instructed the Eastern Congregation. Pius XII, in his first letter, *Summi pontificatus*, recommended the "unity, which is the hope of so many noble minds separated from Us, who yet in their hunger and thirst for justice and peace turn their eyes to the See of Peter from whom they await guidance and counsel" (October 20, 1939, *AAS* 31 [1939], 476). As to relations with "religious leaders of the schismatics," the congregation recommended to the delegate to use all "circumstances … , in order to dispel prejudices and bring righteous souls to the Catholic truth," as well, that it was desirable and useful that the Catholic religious leaders have meetings with the dissident leaders which went beyond polite exchanges, but while avoiding giving scandal to the faithful and protecting the dignity of the Catholic hierarchy" (letter of the Congregation for the Oriental Churches, no. 283/39, dated May 10, 1939, in NA deposit Iraq in ASV).

45. Letter no. 116/444, dated May 4, 1940, in NA deposit Iraq in ASV.

In Iraq, which was not directly affected by World War II, the activities of the Church continued without any particular problems; de Jonghe, true to his mission as the pope's representative, had easy access to Italian and German prison camps, and he also visited the many Polish soldiers who were stationed only sixty kilometers from Baghdad. To all of these he brought spiritual comfort and small gifts, as well as carried news of relatives when he could.

In 1947 the bishop oversaw the succession of Patriarch Yousuf VI Emmanuel Thomas, who had ruled the Chaldean Church for forty-seven years. The new patriarch, Yousuf VII Ghanima (1947–58), was an excellent and pious man; under him the patriarchal see followed the delegation from Mosul to Baghdad, where fifty thousand Chaldeans had taken up residence—not only to escape the difficulties of life in Kurdistan, but also for the job opportunities that the kingdom's capital city offered.[46] The new patriarch, Ghanima, found the Chaldean Church in what he called an "alarming state" of disorder; and he worked to restore it to an acceptable level of efficiency. By his death, at least all of the diocese had bishops assigned to them, and some, such as Baghdad and Mosul, now had auxiliary bishops to help meet their pastoral needs. In November of 1946, the apostolic delegate visited the northern regions of Iraq on the occasion of the consecration of the church in Qaraqosh, a town of Syro-Catholics not far from the ancient city of Assur. He then went to Dehoc, where a new church building had been completed, and to Aqra, where a site had been selected for the construction of a church and a school. While on this northern tour, he expressed his admiration for the simple and warm faith of the Christians of the

46. According to the census conducted in 1947, out of a total Iraqi population of 6,946,000, Baghdad accounted for 550,000, and the Christian communities 139,500. See International Bank for Reconstruction and Development, *The Economic Development of Iraq* (Baltimore: Johns Hopkins University Press, 1952), 126.

ancient Assyrian plain; and he visited the seminaries of Mosul, both patriarchal and inter-ritual, as well as the Dominican mission and Benedict XV's orphanage.

In June 1947, Pius XII transferred de Jonghe to Indonesia, as the first representative to that newly independent country. Upon his departure, after nine years of service, the bishops of Iraq deeply regretted the loss of one who had served with the spirit of a loving father and a prudent and active agent of the Church. Taking his leave of Mesopotamia, de Jonghe wrote to Cardinal Tisserant that the daily work of the papal representative required him to "deal with the [local] mentality, traditions, customs, temperaments, and a variety of rites, and their completing interests, so different from those Europeans, and which demand prudence, patience, gentleness, firmness, and a singular fortitude."[47] The archbishop left the delegation in the hands of the Latin archbishop of Baghdad, Armand-Etienne M. Blanquet du Chayla, who immediately was appointed apostolic delegate on November 20, 1948.[48] In his twenty-six years of service—ten as ordinary of the Latin Church (1938–48) and sixteen serving in both offices (1948–64)—du Chayla applied himself to the roles with competence and dedication. While working for the benefit of the Christian community, and despite his French nationality, he maintained good relations with the Iraqi authorities. The war years had brought political stability to the country, despite some Kurdish uprisings, which were summarily crushed. When the war ended, the country began the earnest work of real independence and of freeing itself from British oversight. It became dis-

47. Letter of the Congregation for Eastern Churches, no. 1776/90, dated August 20, 1947, in NA deposit Iraq in ASV.
48. He would resign both offices on June 1, 1964, becoming the titular archbishop of Dercos. The Frenchman had expressed his strong desire to end his days in Iraq, where he had spent most of his pastoral ministry and where he loved both the climate and the people.

tinctly pro-Arab in its national sentiments,[49] further fueled by a sense of indignation on behalf of the Palestinians following the creation of the state of Israel. Iraq, with the other Arab nations, immediately declared war, and invaded the refounded Israel on May 14, 1948, but met with humiliating defeat.[50] The "Palestinian issue" proceeded to be the touchstone for anti-Semitic sentiments, while the military defeat was the cause of revenge attacks and new persecutions against Jews living in the country.[51] The newly independent Iraq joined the neutral international front and expressed its admiration for the USSR, which offered commercial and military aid. The republic replaced the monarchy following General Kassel's coup, and he chose an international policy of nonalignment and declared Iraqi sovereignty over Kuwait and the Iranian side of the Shatt al-Arab.

The years that followed were marked by further instability and turmoil, including another Kurdish uprising in autumn of 1961,[52] and the subsequent civil war, which created serious problems for the Christians of that region: it is estimated that fifteen thousand abandoned their villages, homes, and belongings in search of refuge in Mosul, Baghdad, and Basra. The three Chaldean dioceses of Amadiya, Aqra, and Zakho were decimated.

49. Even before the end of the war, Prime Minister Nuri al-Saïd was mulling over the formation of an Arab federation of Iraq, Syria, Lebanon, Palestine, and Transjordania, which would operate under Qur'anic law (see *Le Saint Siège et la guerre modiale, Janvier 1944–Mai 1945*, vol. 11 of *Actes et Documents du Saint Siège relatifs à la Seconde Guerre Mondiale*, ed. P. Blet et al. [Vatican City: Libreria Editrice Vaticana, 1981], 100).

50. The other participating nations were Syria, Egypt, Jordan, and Lebanon.

51. Iraq was home to 120,000 Jews; 38,000 of them had fled by 1951, and 70,000 had sought government permission to leave. The response of Nuri al-Saïd's government was to confiscate all their property.

52. Letter of the apostolic nunciature in Iraq, no. 9181/444 dated January 12, 1962, in NA deposit Iraq in ASV). Mala Mustafa Barzani called for an autonomous Kurdistan in northern Iraq by seizing control along the border with Turkey and Iran.

Even the cave-monastery of St. Ormisda was not spared—the abbot was arrested, tortured, and sentenced to twenty years in prison on charges of collaborating with the Kurds. The bishop of Zakho, Thomas Reis, was also arrested and sentenced to one year in prison, commuted to deportation; the bishops of Amadiya and Aqra fled into temporary exile in Rome. In February 1963 Colonel Abd al-Salam Arif overthrew Qasim, who was killed along with numerous communists; and the Ba'ath party came to power, with its socialist and Arab-unionist platform. In four years, there had been two coups. Nevertheless, the country was beginning to know a remarkable economic prosperity resulting from the exploitation of oil. As the apostolic delegate wrote to Rome, oil "carved a river of gold through the country."[53] In the beginning of 1964, the war against the Kurds ended, and a truce was established between the parties. On May 3, 1964, a provisional Iraqi constitution was drafted, which declared the country a "democratic socialist republic" based on the principles of its "Arab and Islamic heritage." The state began to build schools, hospitals, roads, new neighborhoods, and nationalized banks (1964), and prepared to take control of private hospitals and educational institutions. Major works were undertaken, mainly within the cities, where, every day, thousands of workers arrived, attracted by the promise of economic growth and an escape from the poverty of the countryside.

Religious life, which was typical in the villages, faced a crisis in the big cities and saw a sharp decline in vocations, although the northern Christian villages continued to be a source of steady vocations despite the urban migration. In education, Catholic schools were a great success, as evidenced by their more than fourteen thousand students. On the pastoral level, as du Chaya noted, there remained a deep lack of solicitude among

53. Letter no. 5524/90, dated February 15, 1955, in NA deposit Iraq in ASV.

the bishops: the care of their clergy was severely lacking (an evil that neither he nor his predecessors had been able to heal). Even the relations between different Christian communities were riven with partisanship and parochialism, often rooted in their own hierarchies; and anything from outside their particular tradition was viewed with suspicion. The largest Christian community remained the Chaldeans, governed by Patriarch Paul II Cheikho, who was elected on December 13, 1958, and had received ecclesiastical communion from Pope John XXIII on March 12, 1959. He was known as a pious man, active in the construction of churches and the establishment of kindergartens and primary schools. He was a pastor who stayed close to his people, and, though he preferred a simple life for himself, he had a high appreciation of his Church, the role of the patriarchy, and its status and authority. Cautious in political matters, he was not always well understood; indeed, political instability, rebellions in Kurdistan, and the sacking of several Christian villages did not make for easy relations with the civil authorities, who demanded support for their centralizing policies while thousands of Chaldeans and Assyrians were forced to flee their native villages. For many families left homeless, landless, jobless, and penniless, the Church was their only support; and du Chayla was often the first to intervene on their behalf.

Patriarch Cheikho, when he was still bishop of Aqra, saw the arrival in Iraq of first the Petits Frères in 1953, and then, in 1955, the Petites Soeurs de Jésus of Charles de Foucauld, as well as the Redemptorists, who had been called in to help teach in the patriarchal seminaries, preach to the people, and give spiritual assistance to the religious houses. In the same period the Jesuits opened Al-Hikmah University (May 5, 1955), an educational institution that, along with Baghdad College, enjoyed the favor and protection of the government and the people for several years, until the day of the unfortunate nationalization of all schools.

The Assyrian Church of the East, during the patriarchate of the young Shimon XXI Ishai—who had been exiled in 1933 and fled to the United States—split in a new schism, in 1964. Some of their bishops had protested the adoption of the Gregorian calendar in the place of the Julian (relative to the calculation of the liturgical celebrations) and created the Ancient Holy Catholic and Apostolic Church of the East, more commonly known as the Ancient Church of the East, which claimed to be the heir of the Church of Seleucia-Ctesiphon and, in 1968, they instituted a separate patriarchate in Baghdad. Thomas Darmo, metropolitan of India, consecrated three of the bishops who elected him as the new patriarch, while the majority of the faithful remained loyal to Shimun XXI Ishai. Following this mess, Shimon finally agreed to return to Iraq, and the Iraqi government decided to rehabilitate him, in return for a declaration of loyalty. The Ba'ath Party, then in power, received him with honor, and a presidential decree recognized him as the supreme leader of the Assyrian community.[54] The authorities hoped that this would help end the conflict with the Kurds and unite the Assyrians; instead, Shimon, after only a short time back in Iraq, left for America. He came back in 1972, but by this point he was hopelessly discredited in the eyes of his people. The ecclesial division persisted, even after the death of Thomas Darmo in 1969; and the Ancient Church of the East elected a new patriarch, Addai II Giwargis, in February of 1970, who was installed in Baghdad. "They have good faithful," said a Chaldean prelate concerning the two communities, "but their hierarchy is in crisis and split!" The division lasts even to the present day, and there remain two Assyrian churches: the minority, who follow Addai II, and the majority, who recognize the current patriarch as Dinkha IV Khanania.[55]

54. This was in 1970. The patriarch met President Ahmed Hassan al-Bakr, resumed his Iraqi nationality and was authorized to reside in the north of the country; nevertheless, he soon returned to the United States.
55. Mar Dinkha was elected in 1976 as the successor of the outgoing Shi-

Returning to the political context, the Iraqi provisional constitution recognized, in those years, that Arabs and Kurds had to live together in one country; and the authorities of the country would not entertain any aspirations to some alternative, such as independence. They were three legal, political parties: the ruling National Democratic Party (NDP), the Democratic Party of Kurdistan (PDK), and the Iraqi Communist Party (PCI). Following his death in February 1963, General Kassem left a legacy of internal discord, inconsistent foreign policy, and a boiling Kurdish separatist movement. The coup brought to power the Ba'ath Party, which was noted for its intolerance of communists. In November, Abd al-Salam Arif assumed full governmental power, and he continued the work of nationalizing all sectors of industry and financial services. Shortly afterward, in April of 1966, a plane crash ended his tenure in office and brought his brother, Abd al-Rahman Arif, to power. He was replaced, in turn, in 1968 by a coup led by General Ahmed Hassan al-Bakr, although the driving force was one Saddam Hussein, then vice-president of the Revolutionary Command Council. With this coup, the Ba'ath Party remained in total control of the country until the fall of Saddam Hussein in 2003. The Ba'athists, who were the party of the "resurrection," were a secular-socialist movement with libertarian and nationalist themes ("unity, freedom, and socialism"), an anti-imperialist vision in foreign policy through friendship with the Soviet Union, and total opposition to Israel. Saddam Hussein became president of the Republic on July 6, 1969. He was a proponent of vicious repression of internal dissidents, which meant any civil organization that resisted government hegemony. Both the Iraqi Communist Party and the Democratic Party of Kurdistan were repressed because of their opposition to the

---

mon XXI Ishai, last of the hereditary patriarchs, who married and had to leave office. In 1975 Shimon was murdered in San Francisco, California, at the hands of a young Assyrian.

Arabization process, which extended to traditionally non-Arab cities and regions like Kirkuk and the Nineveh Plain. He also expelled what few Jews had managed to remain in Iraq, and he extradited forty thousand Shi'ites to Iran in 1980.

Saddam Hussein signed an agreement with the Kurds in 1970 that was meant to grant some measure of autonomy for the region; but tensions never really relaxed, and the deal was never honored. Finally, in 1974, the agreement was denounced by the Kurds, and about forty thousand peshmerga (Kurdish military forces) prepared to fight the Baghdad regime. Following their brutal suppression, their leader, Mala Mustafa Barzani, left his role to his son Masoud, while Jalal Talabani created the Patriotic Union of Kurdistan (PUK) in the Sulaymaniyah province, bordering Iran. During the 1970s and 1980s, the Iraqi Kurds lived through extreme repression and, in some cases, outright genocide.[56] The violent process of Arabization also extended to the Christian villages, many of which had been reduced in number by expulsion or migration; some of them were almost deserted. Those who remain now recall those years with pain and deep sorrow, remembering the destruction of entire families and communities.

The bellicose attitude of the regime, which paid no heed to the suffering inflicted on its own people, started another war, this time with Iran (1980–88), over the lingering question of sovereignty of the Shatt al-Arab, which was contested by the two countries. Saddam Hussein, abrogating the Algiers Accord,[57] claimed total sovereignty over the waterway and occupied a large area to the east. It was a long and bloody war, and the Ira-

56. The villages of Halabja, Haladin, Bergalou, and Chinara were attached with chemical weapons and have become a grizzly symbol of Saddam's regime. From 1974 to 1990, the war against the Kurds claimed thousands of victims (see M. Galletti, *Iraq*, 70).

57. This was a bilateral pact, concluded in March of 1975, between the shah of Persia, Reza Pahlavi, and Saddam Hussein. It was part of wider negotiations which included the agreements of June 13 and December 26, 1975, about Kurdish separatism.

nian response, led by the regime of Ayatollah Khomeini, was unexpectedly formidable. The long war carried heavy economic consequences for the wider world and led to a global increase in the price of oil. The conflict drew in other Arab nations, which were concerned about the ideology of the Iranian leadership; the European powers and the United States were on one side, and China, the Soviet Union, and other communist countries were on the other supporting Iran. In Iraq, Kurdish separatists, still embittered by the recent persecutions, sought to exploit the government's military preoccupation with Iran. This fueled increased tensions and acts of revenge. For the Iraqi people, those were hard years of destruction, death, economic crises, and lack of security and development. No part of the country was spared, no community was immune from suffering; and the great number of deaths seemed only to strengthen, in some perverse way, a form of unity behind the Ba'athist regime, which was generous to its friends and ruthless to its enemies. In 1988, the UN Security Council condemned both Iraq and Iran, prompting the parties to agree a cease fire and to restore the *status quo ante* (1990). The war saw 400,000 dead, 750,000 wounded, and 70,000 humiliated prisoners. Iraq was left with an enormous financial debt of eighty billion dollars, fourteen billion of which were owed to Kuwait, which took the opportunity to rethink its boundaries with their bellicose neighbor. This separate border dispute itself dated back to the creation of the Iraqi state, which had claimed Kuwait as a province. The Emirate of Kuwait, as a state entity, was a British creation, kept under British sovereignty until June 19, 1961. The lingering claims of Iraqi sovereignty had never been addressed and reemerged as a result of disputes over the large oil reserves in the contiguous subsoils; this gave rise to a serious and escalating conflict. The falling cost of oil, after the end of the war with Iran, caused huge losses in Iraq, preventing them from kick-starting a quick economic recovery.

On August 2, 1990, Saddam Hussein, believing that the United States was not opposed, launched an invasion of Kuwait, occupying it for seven months and arousing the strong reaction of the United Nations. The UN Security Council, with resolution number 660, demanded the withdrawal of the invading forces and, in resolution no. 678, authorized the liberation of Kuwait from military occupation (resolution no. 678). The military and economic sanctions imposed on Iraq (resolution no. 661) were particularly felt by the average people of the country who shouldered the brunt of the effects. The United States, leading a coalition of thirty-five states under the aegis of the United Nations, took the lead in the first Gulf War and eventual took control of the country following the second Gulf War and the fall of the Ba'athist regime in 2003.

4. The Fall of Saddam Hussein

From the time of the war with Iran, and more so following the first Gulf War, Saddam Hussein began to lose his hold on the people, who were themselves unable to get rid of him. During his twenty-five years in power, he had started needless wars, fomented hatred, and halted general social progress. The *rais* (supreme leader)—as he was called—lived a totally segregated life, suspicious of everyone and resigned to his general international discredit. His family, and especially his children, were violent and repressive, and were hated and feared by the population. Once he reasserted his power, which had faltered after the ill-fated adventure in Kuwait, he renewed his heavy-handed suppression of Shi'ite rebels—who had become emboldened by the apparent weakness of the regime—and the ever unruly Kurds, who once again asserted their will to liberate their land from the military control of Baghdad (March 1991). The harsh reaction of the Iraqi army became the source of a new military crisis: UN resolution no. 688 (April 5, 1991) called for international "humanitarian intervention," which saved thousands of lives, and imposed the so-called no-fly zone north of the 36th parallel and south of the 32nd parallel. The Anglo-American defense of Kurdistan gave birth to a sort of protectorate in the northeast of Iraq, while the elections of 1992 provided the establishment of the Regional Assembly of the Autonomous Kurdistan, a parliament with fifty seats allocated to PDK, fifty for the PUK and five for the Assyrian-Chaldeans. With such a political prerequisite, and the assembly's decision for "federal union within a parliamentary democracy in Iraq" (1992), Kurdistan politically pointed the way it intended to go and took charge of its own economic development. The fall of Saddam Hussein followed the occupation of Iraq by military forces—by the United States and Britain, joined by other allied countries—in the second Gulf War. From the time of the liberation of Kuwait, the United States maintained an attitude of open conflict and controversy toward Saddam Hussein over his lack of cooperation with UN sanctions on nuclear, chemical, biological, and missile disarmament by Iraq. United Nations sanctions, in fact, had done nothing to prevent Baghdad from maintaining a large conventional military apparatus, which it brandished with great theatricality at its neighboring countries and at Israel. This situation lasted ten years, but was finally broken by the events of September 11, 2001.[58] Saddam Hussein was quickly suspected by the Bush administration as a possible culprit. But it was felt that this "charge" was a pretext, as was the false charge that Iraq had obtained supplies of uranium from Niger and possessed chemical and biological weapons. By 2002, the will of the Bush administration, and British prime minister Tony Blair, was clear: they wanted to remove Saddam Hussein, who was also opposed

58. The horrific terrorist attacks on the twin towers in New York, the Pentagon in Washington, D.C., and in Pennsylvania, by members of al-Qaeda, put the whole world in suspense.

by Israel, whose annihilation Hussein frequently called for. While France and Russia criticized any form of military intervention, the United States and its allies advanced the doctrine of "preventive war," which was opposed by the Catholic Church, and especially by Pope St. John Paul II. The "nice face" of this theory implied that it was necessary to bring democracy to the country. While trying to mobilize opposition to the invasion internationally, President Saddam Hussein tried to initiate a hasty internal reform, suggesting he step aside and pass power to his son Qusay, in a move not dissimilar to that made by Syrian president Hafez al-Assad and his son Bashar al-Assad (2000), and in Jordan by King Hussein and his son Abdullah II (1999).

Kurdistan supported the allied military intervention and so did Kuwait and the other Arab Gulf countries; Turkey, Jordan, and Syria were less supportive. Saddam Hussein sought ways out of the international military pressure, but he did not want to make any meaningful concessions. He understood that, having deployed a strong military coalition, the United States and its allies were now ready to launch an attack. Saddam Hussein tried his contacts in Jordan; even the apostolic nunciature in Baghdad received emissaries asking for help. He was advised to ban all weapons of mass destruction. Hussein pushed through a measure to this effect by the council of tribal leaders in forty-eight hours; he indicated a willingness to concede to whatever demands the United States might ultimately make, but he excluded the possibility of his own removal. Despite the two peace-seeking missions sent by John Paul II to Washington and Baghdad, the United States was firm in its resolve to attack Iraq, and the pope's attempt at peace was unsuccessful. Not even the stern warning of the saint-pope could deter President George W. Bush from his purpose. Other states in the coalition lined up without too many obstacles. It was to be war. On March 19, 2003, it began; a very sad day for Iraq and for the whole world.

Operation Iraqi Freedom officially lasted forty-two days. On May 1, formal conflict ceased, but not the military occupation. The country itself was plunged into the most violent and chaotic mess: humiliation, revenge, theft, looting, arson, and sacking of public and private buildings threw Iraq into the darkest period of its whole existence. Operation Iraqi Freedom was, thanks to modern media, a war broadcast worldwide. Sophisticated weapons, powerful, and laser-guided to the most sensitive targets of Iraqi power, were deployed, but still claimed the lives of countless innocents. Many domestic opposition forces joined the occupants: Kurds, Shi'ites, political opponents, elements from Kuwait (bent on avenging the Iraqi invasion of ten years before), and many Iraqi exiles returned to lead the "new" Iraq.

Hussein himself was captured, put on trial, and hanged on November 5, 2006. His two sons, Uday and Qusay, were killed in Mosul during a firefight on July 22, 2003; many other senior regime officials were tried and later convicted and hanged. Despite enormous efforts to restore an acceptable level of civil and political life to Iraq, in recent years the country has remained one of the most inhospitable places on earth: fierce persecution of Christians; blood feuds between Shi'ites and Sunnis; attacks against the police and politicians; inability of political leaders to give structure to the country; fragility across all institutions; inefficiency in the new armed forces; immense corruption; an unproductive economy based only on the extraction of oil; emigration of the best and most educated part of the population; lack of confidence in the future. International ambitions and domestic rivalries have combined to form the toxic mixture that is modern Iraq. Iraq is a very beautiful country, with a population fond of the simplicity of life and who can live and progress in good when not subjected to the oppression and instigation of figures like Hussein. The question, therefore, arises: will there be a peaceful future for Iraq?

Chapter 5

The Holy See and Iraq

1. In Defense of Peace and Human Rights

For the past fifty years, the Holy See's engagement with the state of Iraq has been dominated by the same themes: encouraging peace, calling for respect for the religious rights of Christians, contributing to the education of young people, defending human rights and freedoms, and promoting inter-religious and ecumenical relations. These principles embody the vision of the Apostolic See, all the more so when one considers how the Catholic Church has articulated her self-image since Vatican Council II (1962–65); an image enshrined in the constitution *Gaudium et spes*, which inspires and sets out the missionary and pastoral role of the Church in the modern world. All the Catholic bishops of Iraq attended the council,[1] as well as some observers of the Assyrian Church of the East. These observers were party to, and witnesses of, the shift in emphasis desired by the council fathers in the Church's relations with states and defense of rights, moving away from the use of force toward the

---

1. Ecclesiastical institutions—parishes, seminaries, religious communities—were involved through prayer, information, and internal debate. The seminary of St. John in Mosul, for example, was given a three-point program: information, prayer, and exchange of ideas, as reported by the then rector, Dominican Fr. Omez, to Gabriel Acacius Cardinal Coussa, secretary of the Congregation for the Eastern Churches.

fostering of the universal value of human rights. The council also invigorated relations with and between the Eastern Catholic Churches: the decree *Orientalium ecclesiarum* reaffirmed their nature and rightful autonomy within the unity of the one Church of Christ. It also reasserted the equality of their different theological, liturgical, and spiritual patrimonies, and underscored the universal Church's duty to preserve, develop, and hand down these riches. The decree also articulated the particular dignity and rights due to the patriarchs who, in communion with Rome, were recognized as the fathers and leaders of their churches. The decree *Unitatis redintegratio*, while reiterating the Church's doctrine concerning non-Catholics as expressed in the constitution *Lumen gentium*, called upon the whole Church to work toward the goal of unity among all Christians. In the Iraqi context, the council produced some immediate effects; in the small Latin Church, for example, the Congregation for the Eastern Churches suppressed the *missio sui iuris* in Mosul, Baghdad, and Basra, and handed their work over to the Latin ordinary. The Chaldean Church was restructured: Mosul was raised to the rank of an archdiocese in 1967, and the ancient seat of Kurdistan in Arbil was restored in 1968; farther north, thought was given to the reordering of the dioceses of Amadia, Aqra, and Zakho, in light of the emigration crisis, and the flight of so many Christians, following conflicts between the military forces of Baghdad and the Kurdish peshmerga.[2]

In October of 1962, a delegation from the Republic of Iraq had participated in the opening of the council and, later, would also be present for the closing ceremonies. It was at that time that conditions became favorable enough for the establishment of diplomatic relations between the Holy See and Iraq, which

2. In July 1969, Kurdish partisans sacked the monastery of Our Lady of Messi (Alqosh), injuring many of the Chaldean monks. The mountain, which opened to the Plain of Mosul, was the epicenter of fighting between the government and the rebels.

were formalized in 1966 with the opening of the apostolic nunciature in Baghdad, recognized as part of the Holy See, and of the Republic of Iraq's embassy to the Vatican. The apostolic delegate in Baghdad, Maurice Perrin,[3] became the first representative to receive diplomatic recognition, while on the Iraqi side, Ambassador Khalil Hashim became the first representative of Iraq at the Holy See.

As pro-nuncio, Perrin initially retained pastoral responsibility of the Latin archdiocese, but only briefly. In 1972, the Holy See disengaged the role of diplomatic representative from any direct local pastoral activity, leaving the papal representative to liaise with the Iraqi government, to support the Catholic bishops in their pastoral duties, and to promote relations between the Holy See and non-Catholics and non-Christians. The Latin archbishop became purely responsible for the Latin dioceses and for direct pastoral collaboration with the other dioceses of the country.

At this time, Iraq was politically infected with Arabism and socialism, and followed an anti-Western foreign policy, especially in the wake of the Six-Day War (1967). This context resulted in a renewed persecution of the ancient Iraqi Jewish community[4] and foreign missionaries as well. The American Jesuits in particular were regarded with prejudice, despite the general appreciation of their educational activity, especially in Baghdad; and,

3. Born at Grenoble on June 30, 1904, Paul-Marie-Maurice Perrin was ordained a priest in 1936. He was elected titular bishop of Utica on June 7, 1947, and consecrated on October 28, 1947, as an auxiliary to the archbishop of Carthage. On October 29, 1953, Perrin was promoted to replace him as the ordinary of the archdiocese. It was in this capacity that Perrin participated in Vatican Council II, during which he served as a member of the preparatory commission De missionibus. In July 1964, he was appointed *prelato nullius* of Tunis. As a diplomat of the Holy See he was awarded the title of *pro-nuncio*.

4. The Jewish community, which in 1945 had numbered 250,000 people, was greatly reduced following the exodus of 1950–51; by 1972 only 600 Jews lived in Iraq.

in August of 1969, Al-Hikmah University and Baghdad College were both closed. This measure proved to be the starting point of a period of profound change affecting the missionary presence in Iraq and the role of the Church in the educational and social fields.

Perrin made this his immediate concern and tried to stem the trend by constantly petitioning the civil authorities on behalf of the missionaries and for the return of the Chaldean bishops, some of whom had been in exile for some time following the war in Kurdistan. Within the Iraqi church, he encouraged the creation of an "inter-ritual bishops' conference" to unify the efforts of the bishops on matters of common interest such as schools, the defense of minorities, relations with the Orthodox and non-Christians, the work of the lay apostolate, the protection of *waqf*,[5] and the acquisition of legal personality for ecclesiastical bodies. The bishops welcomed the creation of the inter-ritual conference as an opportunity to overcome the age-old segregated mentality that existed among the Churches and remedy their common disorder and lack of mutual undertakings. Perrin also raised the vexed question of the reform of priestly formation. He revived the idea of creating a single major seminary in Baghdad, with two minor seminaries in Baghdad and Mosul. His aspiration was to ensure to all priests, without distinction of rite, received a solid cultural, theological, and pastoral formation, and to create the conditions for ongoing collaboration between the different Churches *sui iuris* (Chaldean, Syrian Catholic, Armenian Catholic, Greek Catholic, and Latin). The French Dominicans, who for a century had been responsible for priestly formation at St. John Seminary, went through a deep vocational crisis and had to reduce their commitment to the seminary. Because

5. *Waqf* is a guarantee that assets for the support of religious communities (Christian, Islamic, and other religions) will be recognized by the government as inalienable.

of this decision, the local Churches were obliged, in line with the encouragement of the council, to assume responsibility for priestly formation.

Perrin left Iraq in 1969. He was succeeded, for a short time, by Archbishop Paolo Mosconi (1970–71)[6] and then, shortly thereafter, by Jean Rupp (1971–78).[7] Meanwhile, the Latin archdiocese was given into the care of the Carmelite Ernest Charles Albert Nyary.[8] Archbishop Rupp was a man of generous and friendly personality. From his arrival, he formed the impression that the Christian community in Iraq was alive and well integrated into the development of the country, and manifested a solid and simple faith, as he wrote in some of his reports of his pastoral visits made in the Plain of Nineveh and in Kurdistan. He noted, however, that the Ba'athist ideology was beginning to take root among some of the clergy, creating discontent and unease among the faithful, and real embarrassment for the hierarchies of the different Churches. As a point of fact: Patriarch

6. Mosconi, a diplomat of the Holy See, was born at Santa Giuletta on September 3, 1914. He was ordained a priest for the diocese of Tortona in 1938. Before coming to Iraq, he had previously been apostolic pro-nuncio in Madagascar. During his short term of office (he retired for health reasons), Iraq adopted a new constitution on July 16, 1970, to replace the provisional constitution of September 21, 1968.

7. Jean-Éduard-Lucien Rupp was born on October 13, 1905, at Saint-Germain-en-Laye, in the diocese of Versailles. He was ordained a priest in 1934, made auxiliary bishop for the archdiocese of Paris on October 28, 1954, and then later promoted the see of the Principality of Monaco. On April 4, 1975, he was made pro-nuncio in Kuwait, following the establishment of diplomatic relations between the emirate and the Holy See.

8. Archbishop Ernest-Marie de Jésus-Hostie Charles Albert Nyary, OCarm, was born on August 30, 1906. He was Hungarian, but a naturalized French citizen. He entered the Carmelites, making his solemn profession on November 1, 1936. He was ordained a priest on May 22, 1937; and in 1954, he became superior of the Carmelite mission in Iraq, a position he held until 1969. A man of great culture, he was elected bishop on March 23, 1972, and consecrated on May 31. The prelate had an excellent understanding of the civil and religious life of the country, and he enjoyed the affection and esteem of all. He served in the role until May 30, 1983.

Cheikho had always maintained a prudent attitude of loyalty to the government, but he was prepared to be critical when he saw the rights of the Church being undermined.[9] It should also be noted that the civil government was itself not above seeking the endorsement of ecclesiastical institutions, or at least their more influential members, and making efforts to appear publicly on good terms with the Church, if only because of the positive international impact that it could have in the West. As one example of the government making a gesture of good will, in October of 1974, the then vice-president Saddam Hussein revoked an expulsion order on all foreign men and women religious, and granted them an immediate residency permit.

The pro-nuncio Rupp was transferred from Iraq to Geneva as the new representative of the Holy See to the Office of the United Nations. He was succeeded by Archbishop Antonio del Giudice (1978–82), a career diplomat, just when the Shatt al-Arab crisis was brewing between the regimes of Saddam Hussein and Ayatollah Khomeini.[10] His four-year term proved to be complex and politically fraught. The Church was trying to secure its autonomy against increasing interference by the regime, and the protection of its freedoms was a constant struggle. The Latin Church, which depended upon foreign clergy, was almost completely compromised when the government decided not to renew the residence visas of foreign religious (February 25, 1980). It was only the prompt intervention of the papal representative that caused the government authorities to suspend and then reverse the decision. There were, however, ongoing rifts caused by

9. He was, for example, publicly and stridently opposed to the civil authorities' attempt to impose the study of the Qur'an on Christian students (1981).

10. Archbishop del Giudice was born at Casoria, near Naples, on April 16, 1913. Ordained a priest in 1936, he entered the diplomatic service of the Holy See in 1940. On April 18, 1962, he was elected titular bishop of Hierapolis in Syria and sent as apostolic delegate to Korea; he also served as papal representative to the Dominican Republic, Venezuela, and Malta.

the nationalization of Catholic schools, the issue of ownership of school buildings confiscated from religious orders, and the mandatory teaching of the Qur'an for religious education, even for Christian pupils. In this oppressive atmosphere, a migration of political dissidents and many Christians began. Repeated wars, police oppression, and lack of basic protection by the rule of law turned this into a steady stream leaving the country. The United States, Canada, Britain, Sweden, and Australia were their preferred destinations and became home to important communities of the Iraqi diaspora; arranging for proper pastoral provision for these communities began to pose an additional problem. In the blistering summer heat of 1982, Archbishop del Giudice died, and Pope John Paul II chose Luigi Conti to succeed him.[11] His mission began with the bloody Iran-Iraq War already underway, with its countless victims mounting, even among the Christian communities. The humanitarian response, ordered by John Paul II, took Cardinal Roger Etchegaray, president of the Pontifical Commission for Justice and Peace, to both Baghdad and Tehran in an attempt to arrange the return of thousands of prisoners, taken by both sides, to their families. It was during Conti's tenure that St. John Seminary in Mosul finally ceased to exist. The withdrawal of the Dominicans from its management, the decay of the property, and the relocation of the seminarians to Baghdad had finally put an end to a brief but worthy history of service to the Iraqi church. The seminary had trained many clerics and served as a center for pastoral and social outreach, and had been a vital contributor to the spiritual life of a large part of the Iraqi clergy.

Conti was succeeded as pro-nuncio by Marian Oles (1988–94), whose term saw the end of the Iran-Iraq War in 1988, and

11. The new pro-nuncio, Conti, was born at Ceprano on March 2, 1929. He was ordained a priest in 1954, and he was promoted to the titular see of Graziana on August 2, 1975. He had previously served as papal representative in Haiti and apostolic delegate in the Antilles.

the invasion of Kuwait in 1990.[12] The new war led to the defeat of Iraq, and the harsh conditions imposed on the country led to a long and painful internal crisis. For the people of Iraq, these were years of anguish: the regime imposed fierce controls, and deprived the people of all prospects of political freedom. Meanwhile, sanctions led to shortages of food and other goods, including medicine; and hospitals ran short of doctors and adequate supplies. For twelve years, Iraq experienced a protracted period of economic, cultural, and social decline, with many young people taking any opportunity to emigrate and escape military conscription and economic hardship. The sanctions, however, did not unseat the Ba'athist regime, and Iraqis adapted to a humble life under tight government control. As pro-nuncio, Oles was one of the few diplomats to remain in Iraq throughout the war, earning local respect and appreciation. The Holy See, while on one the hand insisting on the re-establishment of international justice (meaning the withdrawal of Iraqi forces from Kuwait), on the other hand demanded that no effort be spared to prevent the burden of defeat and the weight of international sanctions falling on the country's innocent population. At the ecclesiastical level, the Church in Iraq, although technically retaining freedom of worship, was greatly limited by the totalitarian regime, which controlled every part of daily life. Meanwhile, after thirty years of governance by Patriarch Cheikho, the Chaldean Church had a new leader in the person of Raphaël I Bidawid (1989), who had been, until his election, bishop of Beirut of the Chaldeans.[13] The Chaldean Church was the most numerous

12. Born at Miastkowo, Poland, on December 8, 1934, he was ordained a priest in 1961. On November 28, 1987, he was elected bishop of the titular see of Raziaria and made pro-nuncio for Iraq and Kuwait.

13. Patriarch Bidawid was born at Mosul on April 17, 1922; he had been a priest since October 22, 1944. He was elected and consecrated for the see of Amadia on October 6, 1957. On March 2, 1966, he was transferred to the see of Beirut of the Chaldeans and elected as patriarch of the Chaldean Church

and influential of the Christian communities, and it preferred to maintain a traditional way of life, though a good part of the clergy was increasingly calling for some form of modernization. During his tenure, Oles welcomed the Missionaries of Charity (Saint Teresa of Calcutta's sisters) to Baghdad. They arrived at the personal invitation of President Saddam Hussein and took over the management of a small home for mentally and physically disabled children.

Oles was, in his turn, succeeded Giuseppe Lazzarotto (1994–2000), who arrived to find a country whose basic civil institutions and services had been deeply compromised by the economic sanctions.[14] The political situation was increasingly tense. Saddam Hussein's regime was rocked by purges and defections of senior officials, including members of his own extended family, whom he showed himself more than willing to eliminate if he considered it necessary.[15] Kurdistan was also in a state of ongoing political-military tension, leaving the population in constant suspense. The two political factions, the DPK (Kurdish Democratic Party) and the PUK (Patriotic Union of Kurdistan), both vied for local political dominance, while maintaining an attitude of open belligerence to the government in Baghdad. In December of 1996, the United Nations and Iraq finally agreed to an "oil for food" program, which enabled the government in Baghdad to sell limited quantities of oil for the purchase of basic necessities for the population (food, medicine, hygiene products). But the ongoing refusal to open up so-called presi-

---

in 1989, receiving ecclesiastical communion from John Paul II on June 11 of that year.

14. Lazzarotto was born at Carpané, in the diocese of Padua, on May 24, 1942. A priest since 1967, he was elected to the titular see of Numana and consecrated archbishop on October 7, 1994.

15. This included General Abd al-Kamel Kassem (1996), a close associate and son-in-law of the president, who, with his statements about weapons of mass destruction, had aggravated tensions among Iraq, the UN, and the United States.

dential sites to UN weapons and nuclear inspections continued to raise the pressure on both sides; in response to an increasingly firm demand for access to the sites, international inspectors were expelled, triggering a new wave of bombings. Finally, with resolution number 1284 (1999), the UN Security Council and Iraq reached a compromise, in an effort to bring some measure of relief to the general Iraqi population, who remained the hardest hit by international sanctions. In the winter of 1999, in preparation for the jubilee pilgrimage of the Holy Year 2000, John Paul II proposed a personal "pilgrimage of peace" to Ur of the Chaldeans, but Saddam Hussein denied him permission to enter Iraq. This was an enormous diplomatic mistake, demonstrating the historical myopia and general paranoia of the regime. In addition to the immediate diplomatic fallout, it served to make Saddam Hussein appear weak and underlined his discredited reputation at the international level.

In the religious sphere, important ecumenical steps were taken in those years toward a better mutual understanding between the Catholic Church and the Assyrian Church of the East. After several years of "unofficial dialogue," increasingly cordial contact led to the establishment of the Joint International Commission for Theological Dialogue, which in turn led to the *Common Christological Declaration* between Pope John Paul II and Patriarch Dinkha IV in 1994,[16] and the joint statement of the patriarchs Bidawid I and Dinkha IV in 1996.[17] This work was re-

16. "Whatever our Christological divergences have been, we experience ourselves united today in the confession of the same faith in the Son of God who became man so that we might become children of God by his grace." Pope John Paul II and Patriarch Dinkha IV, "Common Christological Declaration Between the Catholic Church and the Assyrian Church of the East," *L'Osservatore Romano*, November 12, 1994. This historic document brought to an end the Christological controversy that had existed between the two Churches since the Council of Ephesus.

17. Patriarch Mar Raphaël Bidawid and Patriarch Mar Dinkha IV, "Joint Patriarchal Statement," *Eastern Churches Journal* 3, no. 3 (1996), 171–73.

inforced the following year by the *Joint Synodal Decree for Promoting Unity* signed by the Chaldean and Assyrian patriarchs.[18] Bonds were further strengthened in October of 2001, with the publication of the document *Guide for the Admission to the Eucharist* between the Assyrian Church of the East and the Chaldean Church, which was jointly authored by the Congregation for the Doctrine of the Faith, the Congregation for the Eastern Churches, and the Pontifical Council for Promoting Christian Unity, and which recognized the validity of the Eucharist of the Assyrian Church of the East.[19] An important event in the Chaldean Church came with the celebration of a special synod in Rome, in June of 2000, in the context of the jubilee year of the new millennium. Pope John Paul II, in receiving the prelates, called upon the Church to set its sights on new, ever broader horizons in its mission to announce the kingdom of God through its own ecclesial traditions. A few months later, Lazzarotto completed his mission as nuncio in Iraq. He was succeeded by me, Archbishop Fernando Filoni (2001–6), whom John Paul II asked to become "a messenger of peace and reconciliation."[20] The country was, in fact, in serious internal and international crisis. The so-called smart sanctions imposed by the United Nations were unable to lift it out of the economic depression into which it had settled. Meanwhile, political oppression and police-state controls were increasingly strict. The UN was unable to accept a "comprehensive dialogue" as the first phase of a "comprehensive

18. Mar Raphaël I Bidawid and Mar Dinkha IV, *Joint Synodal Decree for Promoting Unity between the Assyrian Church of the East and the Chaldean Catholic Church*, August 15, 1997.

19. Congregation for the Doctrine of the Faith, Congregation for the Eastern Churches, and Pontifical Council for Promoting Christian Unity, "Guide for the Admission to the Eucharist," *Information Service*, no. 108 (2001/IV), 148 and following.

20. Born at Manduria (Taranto) in 1946, I was ordained a priest on July 3, 1970, for the diocese of Nardò (Lecce); John Paul II promoted me to the titular see of Volturnum and consecrated me bishop on March 19, 2001.

settlement" for the whole matter, and the atmosphere that was created seemed destined to lead to military conflict. Even the Christian community found itself under renewed pressure from the government, which was becoming markedly more Islamic in its attitudes, quite putting aside the secular origins of Ba'athism. The shift in tone to an Islamic populism sought support among the masses through measures such as forbidding Christians parents to give their children "un-Arab" names, canceling travel and identity documents for Christian religious,[21] and attempting to reintroduce the study of the Qur'an for Christians in schools. Despite the dire economic straits the country was in, the regime spent huge sums building monumental mosques, while in Mosul there were repeated instances of intimidation against churches, clergy, and faithful by Sunni Wahhabis.

The "preventive war"[22] of the United States and its allies began on March 19, 2003; it was short and destructive. The military and political structure dissolved with the fall of Baghdad on April 9. The Church, through its own structures, was ready and willing to give hospitality and relief: sacred buildings were opened to both Christians and Muslims, water and food were shared. The institutions of the Church, and their ministers, both local and international, were exemplary in their courage and dedication. On April 29, Iraq's bishops unanimously called for the future political system of the country to respect democratic

21. Civil recognition of Christians was totally removed, and they were reclassified as "non-Muslims." The government feared that Christian names would make it easier for them to emigrate to the West. Religious designation and recognition of Muslims remained the same.

22. In an editorial published in their January 18, 2003, *La Civiltà Cattolica* gave a detailed commentary on the concept, titled "No a una guerra 'preventiva' contro l'Iraq" ("No to a 'Preventive' War against Iraq"), which articulated the dangers of the U.S. administration's reasoning and how it was morally unacceptable. In 1991, John Paul II had already warned President Bush senior, on the occasion of the first war against Iraq, that "War is an adventure with no return."

principles and to recognize the religious, cultural, social, and political rights of Christians: asking not for special privileges, they said, but prevention of discrimination. The elderly Patriarch Bidawid, who was seriously ill, died at Lebanon in July of 2003. On December 3 of the same year, he was succeeded by Emmanuel III Delly, to whom John Paul II immediately granted ecclesiastical communion.[23] As a gesture of great solidarity and recognition of the sufferings of the Church and of the Iraqi people, Pope Benedict XVI made him a cardinal in the consistory of November 24, 2007. He was the first Chaldean patriarch, and native Iraqi, to join the College of Cardinals. Because of his health, he resigned from office on December 19, 2012, and was succeeded on January 31, 2013 by Louis Raphaël I Sako, who received ecclesiastical communion on February 1, 2013.[24]

2. What Iraq?

The end of the Ba'athist regime and its leader did not bring peace to Iraq. The ensuing military occupation triggered a spiral of hatred and reprisals, which led, with the support of terrorist forces, to protracted urban warfare and armed resistance. In

23. Born at Telkaif (Iraq) on September 27, 1927, Delly was ordained a priest on December 21, 1952. During Vatican Council II he was elected titular bishop of Paleopololi in Asia, and appointed as auxiliary to the patriarch, he received his episcopal consecration on April 19, 1963. On May 6, 1967, he was promoted to the titular see of Kaskar, and served as a curial archbishop, first to Patriarch Cheikho and then Patriarch Bidawid. He gave up the patriarchal office, retiring to private life, on December 19, 2012, and died on April 9, 2014. Following the fall of the regime of Saddam Hussein, he had declared: "Politically we have been liberated from the old regime, but in fact we are now under occupation. And the people, as would any people, do not like it." He witnessed the most difficult moments suffered by his Church, and of the Iraqi people, through the innumerable terrorist attacks that claimed the lives of so many Christians.

24. Born at Zakho, in Iraqi Kurdistan, on July 4, 1948, Sako was ordained a priest in 1974, and elected archbishop of Kirkuk of the Chaldeans on September 27, 2003, before finally being elected to the patriarchal see.

the years following the second Gulf War, Iraq has become an unlivable country. Kidnapping and murder are commonplace for both foreigners and Iraqis, military officials and journalists, humanitarian and economic workers, politicians and religious leaders, women and children. The world, through the media, has experienced the horror of the gruesome beheadings of innocent people, or other cold-blooded means of execution, as well as the campaign of devastating attacks against political and diplomatic institutions, and the police. Even churches and mosques have not been spared. Iraq has become a country without laws and at the mercy of political terrorists, criminals, and pseudo-religious armed gangs.

Groups of Sunni Arabs (many of whom bitterly resent their fall from power, which they saw pass through the occupying forces to the Shi'ites and the Kurds), as well as sectarian Shi'ites, former Ba'athists, members of al Qaida, and mere common criminals—all well supplied with weapons, explosives, and money, and enjoying complicity at various levels of the new government—have sorely tested first the occupying forces and then the newly trained police force. Reliable information reports that, from 2004 to 2009, victims of terrorist attacks and violent crimes totaled 109,032—of which 66,081 were civilians, 23,984 terrorists, 15,196 Iraqi soldiers, and 3,771 military allies.[25] The destruction has been endless. Baghdad has been fragmented by high walls, roadblocks, red zones, and green zones, and subjected to endless prohibitions and controls. With little electricity, no running aqueducts or sewers, severed telephone lines, scarce oil supplies, and impassable and dangerous roads, the capital and the country suffered an urban and institutional collapse. Yet in those dark days, in the heart of what was once known as "the citadel of Saddam," the first constitutional act of a democratic government took place,

---

25. See M. Galletti, *Iraq, il cuore del mondo* (Rome: Edizioni Labrys, 2011), 94.

ad interim, in July 2004, which guided the country to free elections on January 30, 2005, and the preparation of a new constitution, which was approved by referendum on October 15, 2005. The Kurdish leader, Jalal Talabani, became the president of the Republic on April 6, 2005; and a parliament and a new government were elected. There was talk of peace, and this seemed a real hope. Alas, it has not become a reality. In fact, institutions have not yet managed to rise to the expectations of a population that yearns for a respectful and peaceful civil coexistence. It is not simply a question of the ongoing campaign of terrorist attacks, but also of bitter political division between the parties. Iraqi democracy has, so far, shown all the flaws and limitations of the country's jagged society. Without stable institutions, there is little hope of creating a coexistence founded upon the rule of law, or of overcoming entrenched partisanship.

Iraq has an important role in the Middle East: religiously, as the cradle of Shi'ism; politically, because it is a strategic link between Iranian Asia and a Middle East containing Israel; economically, because of its enormous oil wealth. Iraq's tilt toward the Sunni Arab world—as historically happened during the years of the kingdom and of the first republic—created strong tensions with its powerful Shi'ite neighbor, Iran, which is also rich in oil and an important strategic neighbor to the Arab countries of the Persian Gulf. With its current tilt toward the Shi'ite world, Iraq is now under pressure from the powerful Sunni community. As the roles have been reversed, one must wonder if this land of Mesopotamia will come to know yet more trials and struggles, as it remains in the sights of its neighbors who may yet turn into new occupiers: as it was throughout its whole history, with the Medes toward the Chaldeans, the Macedonians toward the Assyrians, Romans to the Parthians, the Arabs toward the Sassanids, the Mongols toward Arabs, and the Ottomans toward the Persian Safavids.

Custody of the most sacred places of Shi'ism is the "big religious factor," and the encapsulation of the Islamic dichotomy that will always be at the heart of Iraq's socio-political tensions. Kufa, Karbala, and Najaf, in fact, are the "sacred" cities for the Shi'ites, and the places of origin of their Islamic confession. Custody has been the cause of repeated terrorist attacks, especially on the occasion of Ashura, carried out against pilgrims by Sunni gangs.[26] These places always will remain a bone of contention between the two major factions that make up the Islamic community.

The history of this conflict dates back to the beginnings of Islam, a few decades after the death of Muhammad (632), when the Arab conquerors of Mesopotamia, defeating the Sassanids, joined their victorious armies in Palestine and Syria, and Damascus became the site the caliphate. The first three men to be elected caliph (Abu Bakr, Omar, and Othman), were considered "usurpers" by the party loyal to the descendants of Muhammad: Ali ibn Abi Talib (656–61), his cousin and son-in-law (who married his daughter Fatima), claimed the political-religious leadership of Islam for himself, in the absence of a direct male heir; his succession would—so he claimed—maintain the line of Muhammad. The *sci'at* (from which the word "Shia" is derived), which is the "party" of Ali, believed that the descendants of Muhammed had the right of succession, and this produced a schism in the *umma*, that is, in the Islamic community. In the struggle between the opposing forces, Ali was defeated at Siffin (on the upper Euphrates); and he took refuge in lower Mesopotamia, where, in 661, he was killed in the mosque of Kufa. His violent death fueled the accession to the Shi'ite branch, which proclaimed him "Ali the saint of Allah." His claims were then taken up by his son

26. Ashura is the Shi'ite season of commemoration of the killing of Imam al-Husain ibn Ali and his followers by the Umayyad caliph Yazid I, lasting forty days.

Husain—born to his wife Fatima—who took charge of the rebellion and was defeated by the superior forces of the Umayyadi in Damascus, and later was killed at Karbala, along with his two sons (Ali Akbar and Ali Aqar), his half-brother, his nephew, and seventy-two of his followers. This occurred on October 10, 680, which is still marked as a Shia penitential celebration in their memory (Ashura). Ali was buried in Najaf, and Husain in Karbala; and their tombs became important pilgrimage destinations. Their deaths consolidated the power of the Umayyad caliphate, while Shi'ism stretched into Persia. There it was welcomed as a reaction to the Umayyadi of Damascus.

The strong religious antagonism that divides the Shi'ite and Sunni communities has also soaked through the politico-sectarian disputes of Iraq, and there is no real line of demarcation to be drawn between the two aspects of the conflict. Karbala and Najaf have always been centers of Shi'ite power, for Iraq and beyond, often setting the region at odds with Sunni political power in Baghdad. These historic tensions are also currently being played out in the conflict between the Shi'ites and the so-called ISIS caliphate. Peace remains impossible until there is a willingness to pass from hatred to tolerance, and until these two communities are willing to respect the right of the other, and of all the religious communities of Iraq, to exist.

3. The Christians of Iraq Today

The Eastern Church is the continuation of the original Christian presence in Iraq. It is a Church, as has been said already, that dates back to the apostolic era, and that lost communion with the other Christian Churches between the fifth and sixth centuries. Its isolation and excesses led to the birth of the Chaldean Church, which today has its patriarchal see in Baghdad,[27]

27. Pope Julius III established the patriarchal see with the bull *Divina*

while the Assyrian Church of the East is headquartered in Chicago. In recent years, under Patriarch Dinkha IV, the Assyrian Church has abolished the hereditary succession of the patriarchal office and eliminated explicitly Nestorian references from their professions. With the *Common Christological Declaration* between the Catholic Church and the Assyrian Church of the East in 1994, doctrinal dialogue has been re-established with the Chaldean Church; and there has been, on the Catholic side, a recognition of the validity of the anaphora used in the Eucharistic liturgy of the Assyrian Church of the East. As for the Ancient Church of the East (with its patriarchal see in Baghdad, created in the 1964 schism of the Assyrian Church of the East), it remains a more properly Nestorian Church and maintains its liturgical use of the Julian calendar. From the numerical point of view, the Chaldean Church remains the largest, with more than a million faithful scattered across Iraq, Europe, the United States, Canada, and Australia; all countries with thriving Assyrian diaspora communities. Alongside these major Christian denominations, there are other Christian communities still living in Iraq, including Syrian Catholics and Orthodox, the Armenian Catholics and Orthodox, Greek Catholics, and Latins.

Despite being a numerical minority, the presence of Christians in Mesopotamia is significant in other ways. Though reduced through generations of persecution and the civil policies of the previous century, Christianity has been a vital part of the culture and traditions of the country. But the question presents itself: will this diverse and rich Christian presence—and this equally applies to other religious minorities—survive the near future, or will it disappear, as did the Jewish community, which once thrived in this land? This question should preoccupy everyone with a benevolent interest in human affairs, or who es-

---

disponente clementia, on April 28, 1553, creating the title of patriarch of Mosul, to which was later added "of the Chaldeans."

teems the culture and role that Christians have played, over two thousand years of history, in the land of Abraham and of numerous prophets—Ezekiel, the seer of the Holy Spirit; Daniel, the wise man; Nahum, the man who conversed with God; and Jonah, the preacher of Nineveh—whose tombs are also venerated by Muslims.

The survival of these communities hinges upon both the central government in Baghdad and the Autonomous Region of Kurdistan valuing them as an integral part of society.[28] But the broader problem is the lack of any certainty about the future of Iraq. Fatigue and fear have taken hold among the people as they look ahead, and they have little experience or expectation of civil and political institutions that goes beyond suspicion and disappointment. While the circumstances are not hopeless, the situation is likely to remain unchanged without internal and international support. Iraq—split between Shi'ites, Sunnis, and Kurds—is economically divided between the rich and the poor, and religiously divided into numerous different confessions. It is a country that cries out for unity and certainty. Christians, as a community, want the unity and the certainty that comes from full citizenship, and not being made a legally reduced minority. But they also need—the Latin archbishop of Baghdad, Jean Benjamin Sleiman, OCD, has written—to be "re-invigorated in the faith" and no longer have to "act like a minority anxiously clinging to a past history. They must rebuild their homeland, with citizenship and a charter of human rights, for the common good and proper organization. The Christians of Iraq are citizens of a great nation, and not a minority imprisoned by their own helplessness."[29] But is this enough?

The mosaic that makes up this land is under serious threat

28. During the occupation of Iraq, from 2003 until today, more than eighty churches and sacred buildings have come under terrorist attack (see S. Rassam, *Christianity in Iraq* [Australia: Freedom Publishing, 2010], 242–47).

29. J. B. Sleiman, *Nella trappola irachena* (Milan: Paoline, 2007). 122.

by the exodus of thousands of people of every creed and social condition. Only peace, real peace, can put an end to it. A united Iraq is a great prize for all its people, for the Middle East, and for the whole world. In this sense it is vital that Christians remain and contribute to its development; they are part of this mosaic. It would also benefit the Muslim world, since, as many have observed, they are a necessary element of moderation, stimulating and appealing to the best parts of the great Iraqi society. For this reason it is essential that they be helped to stay in their homeland, helped to believe that there is a place for them there. "Iraqi Christians," wrote President Muhammad Fuad Masum to Pope Francis, "have always been part of the living conscience of the community, and, through this, were extraordinary messengers in bringing the message of Our Lord Jesus Christ and, as citizens, participants in manifesting the human nature of the Iraqi people: of Iraq as a person, characterized by the values of goodness, love and peace."[30]

A modern Iraq, full of history, of possibility and responsibility (not least because of its huge oil resources, which continue to be a source of discord, jealousy, envy, and oppression) should be defended, helped, and supported more than ever. But the first responsibility belongs to Iraq's three great communities—Shi'ites, Sunnis, and Kurds—to desire and allow the Muslim, the Christian, the Yazidi, the Mandeo, and all the other minorities in the country, to return to their country and to contribute to, and live in, peace. Let us not forget:

The history of this earth is a network of people and events, and those of today cannot be separated from those of yesterday. Certain aspects seem to repeat themselves: the invasion of Mesopotamia, the terrible wars that have soaked her in blood, the despots who have

---

30. Letter from President Muhammad Fuad Masum of October 2014, in response to the papal message delivered by Cardinal Filoni to President Fuad Masum.

raped her, the lusts that have devoured her. The highs and lows, destruction and looting, kidnappings and ransoms, love and death: all have existed here forever! The Bible speaks of it, so do the ruins, so does the screaming of the sandstorms, it is written in books and in today's news.[31]

Does a brighter future await this country and her people? That is yet to be seen.

31. F. Filoni, *La Chiesa nella terra di Abramo* (Milan, Italy: BUR Biblioteca Universale Rizzoli, 2008), 12–13.

⇒ Bibliography

A Chronicle of the Carmelites in Persia and the Papal Mission of the XVIIth and XVIIIth centuries. 2 vols. London: Eyre and Spottis-woode, 1939.

Acta Apostolicae Sedis (AAS). Commentarium officiale. 107 vols. Vatican City: Libreria Editrice Vaticana, 1909–2015.

Acta Santae Sedis (ASS). Commentarium officiale. 41 vols. Vatican City: Libreria Editrice Vaticana, 1865–1908.

Annales de l'Archevêché de Bagdad rédigées par mgr. Lion, A. de B. (Administrateur de Babylone). In the archives of the apostolic nunciature to Iraq, Vatican Secret Archives.

Artifoni, Enrico, et al. *Storia medievale.* Rome: Donzelli Editore, 1998.

Babo, I. R. *La storia dei cristiani in Iraq.* In Arabic. Baghdad, 1948.

Badr, Habib, ed. *Christianity. A History in the Middle East.* Beirut, Lebanon: Middle East Council of Churches, 2005.

Beaumont, I. M. *Christology in Dialogue with Muslims: A Critical Analysis of Christian. Presentations of Christ for Muslims from the Ninth and Twentieth Centuries.* Oregon: Regnum, 2005.

Bello, E. *La Congrégation de Saint Hormisdas et l'Église Chaldéenne dans la première moité du siècle XIXe.* In *Orientalia Christiana Analecta,* no. 122. Rome, 1939.

Beltrami, G. *La Chiesa Caldea nel secolo dell'Unione.* In *Orientalia Christiana,* no. 83. Rome, 1933.

Benedict XVI, Pope. General audience, November 21, 2007. http://w2.vatican.va/content/benedict-xvi/en/audiences/2007/documents/hf_ben-xvi_aud_20071121.html.

Bidawid, Mar Raphaël, and Mar Dinkha IV. "Joint Patriarchal Statement." *Eastern Churches Journal* 3, no. 3 (1996): 171–73.

Bidawid, Mar Raphaël I, and Mar Dinkha IV. *Joint Synodal Decree for Promoting Unity between the Assyrian Church of the East and the Chaldean Catholic Church.* August 15, 1997.

Blet, P. *La Seconda Guerra Mondiale negli Archivi Vaticani*. Italian translation by Fr. E. P. Pacelli, ed. R. Di Castro. Rome: San Paolo, 1999.

Blet, P., et al., eds. *Le Saint Siège et la guerre en Europe, Mars 1939– Août 1940*. Vol. 1 of *Actes et documents du Saint Siège relatifs à la Seconde Guerre Mondiale*. Vatican City: Libreria Editrice Vaticana, 1970.

———, eds. *Le Saint Siège et la guerre en Europe, Novembre 1942– Décembre 1943*, vol. 7 of *Actes et documents du Saint Siège relatifs à la Seconde Guerre Mondiale*. Vatican City: Libreria Editrice Vaticana, 1973.

———, eds. *Le Saint Siège et la guerre modiale, Janvier 1944–Mai 1945*. Vol. 11 of *Actes et Documents du Saint Siège relatifs à la Seconde Guerre Mondiale*. Vatican City: Libreria Editrice Vaticana, 1981.

———, eds. *Le Saint Siège et les victimes de la guerre, Janvier–Decembre 1943*. Vol. 9 of *Actes et documents du Saint Siège relatifs à la Seconde Guerre Mondiale*. Vatican City: Libreria Editrice Vaticana, 1975.

Bobone, P. G., A. Mengozzi, and M. Tosco, eds. *Linguistic and Oriental Studies in Honour of Fabrizio A. Pennacchietti*. Wiesbaden: Harrassowitz, 2006.

Bosio, Guido. *Iniziazione ai Padri*. Vol. 2. Turin: Società Editrice Internazionale, 1964.

Bracket, D. "Executive Officer Apostolic Annex." In *Catholic Encyclopedia*. Vatican City: 1950.

Campanile, G. *Storia della regione del Kurdistan*. Napoli: Stamperia dei fratelli Fernandes, 1818.

Caretto, G., G. Corm, G. Crespi, J-D. Forest, C. Forest, and J. Ries. *Iraq—Dalle antiche Civiltà alla barbarie del mercato del petrolio*. Milan: Jaca Book, 2003.

Charles-Roux, F. *France et chrétiens d'Orient*. Paris: Flammarion, 1939.

Chevalier, M. *Les Montagnardes chrétiens du Hakkari et du Kurdistan septentrional*. Paris: Publications du Departement de geographie de l'Universite de Paris-Sorbonne, 1985.

Comunità di Sant'Egidio. *I Cristiani in Medio Oriente tra futuro, tradizione e islam*. Milan: Leonardo International, 2009.

Cuinet, Vital. *La Turquie d'Asie—Géographie Administrative*. Vol. 2. Paris: Ernest Leroux, 1891.

Dann, U. *Iraq under Qassem: A Political History, 1958–1963.* Jerusalem: Israel Universities Press, 1969.

de Dreuzy, Agnes. *The Holy See and the Emergence of the Modern Middle East: Benedict XV's Diplomacy in Greater Syria, 1914–1922.* Washington, D.C.: The Catholic University of America Press, 2016.

Del Zanna, G. *I cristiani e il Medio Oriente (1798–1924).* Bologna: Il Mulino, 2011.

Dinkha IV, Patriarch, and Pope John Paul II. "Common Christological Declaration between the Catholic Church and the Assyrian Church of the East." *L'Osservatore Romano,* November 12, 1994.

Etheria. *The Pilgrimage of Etheria,* translated by M. L. McClure and C. L. Feltoe. London: Society for Promoting Christian Knowledge, 1919.

Eugene IV, Pope. *Benedictus sit Deus.* Bull. August 7, 1445.

Eusebius of Caesarea. *Ecclesiastical History.*

————. *Vita Constantini.*

Fiey, J-M. *Communautés syriaques en Iran et Irak des origines à 1552.* London: Variorum Reprints, 1979.

————. *Jalons pour une histoire de l'Église en Irak.* Vol. 310, subsidia 36, of *Corpus Scriptorum Christianorum Orientalium.* Louvain: Peeters Publishers, 1970.

Filoni, Fernando. *La Chiesa nella terra di Abramo,* Milan, Italy: BUR Biblioteca Universale Rizzoli, 2008.

Galanus, Clemens. *Conciliationis Ecclesiae Armenae cum Romana.* Vol. I, 2. Rome: Congregatio de Propaganda Fide, 1658.

Galletti, Mirella. *Iraq, il cuore del mondo.* Rome: Edizioni Labrys, 2011.

————. *Le Kurdistan et ses chrétiens.* Paris: Editions du Cerf, 2010.

Garzoni, Maurizio. *Grammatica e vocabolario della lingua kurda composti dal padre Maurizio Garzoni de' Predicatori ex-missionario apostolico.* Roma: Sacra Congregazione di Propaganda Fide, 1787.

Gefaell, Pablo. "Las Iglesias orientales antiguas ortodoxas y católicas." In *Las Iglesias orientales,* ed. Adolfo González Montes, 595–643. Madrid: Biblioteca de Autores Christiana, 2000.

Giamil, S. *Genuinae relationes inter Sedem Apostolicam et Assyriorum Orientalium seu Chaldaeorum Ecclesia.* Rome: E. Loescher, 1902.

Habbi, Joseph. "La Chiesa d'Oriente in Mesopotamia." *Mesopotamia* 27 (1992): 207–24.

Histoire de l'Archevêché. In the archives of the apostolic nunciature to Iraq, Vatican Secret Archives.

Impagliazzo, M. *Una finestra sul massacro—Documenti inediti sulla strage degli armeni (1915–1916).* Milan: Guerini e Associati, 2004.

International Bank for Reconstruction and Development. *The Economic Development of Iraq.* Baltimore: Johns Hopkins University Press, 1952.

Jewish Agency for Palestine, Economic Research Institute. *Statistical Handbook of Middle Eastern Countries.* Jerusalem: D. B. Aaronson, 1945.

Korolevshij, C. "Audo (Joseph) (1948–1978)." In *Dictionnaire d'Histoire et Géographie Ecclésiastique,* vol. 5, coll. 317–56. Paris: Letouzey et Ané, 1931.

Legrand, Hervé, and Giuseppe Maria Croce. *L'Œuvre d'Orient— Solidarités anciennes et nouveaux défis.* Paris: Cerf, 2010.

Leo XIII, Pope. Apostolic letter *Ad sinum.* July 31, 1902.

Le Quien, Michel. *Oriens christianus, in quattuor patriarchatus digestus; ecclesiae patriarchae, caeterique praesules totius orientis.* Vol. 3. Paris: Typographia Regia, 1740.

Lesourd, Paul. *Histoire des missions catholiques.* Paris: Librairie de l'Arc, 1937.

Martina, Giacomo. *Pio IX (1851–1866).* Vol. 51. Rome: Gregorian University Press, 1986.

Missions Catholiques, Les. *Bulletin Hebdomadaire Illustré de l'Œuvre de la Propagation de la Foi.* Lyon: Bureau des Missions Catholiques.

Montgomery, J. A. *The History of Yaballaha III and of His Vicar Bar Sauma.* Piscataway, N.J.: Gorgias Press, 2006.

"No a una guerra 'preventiva' contro l'Iraq." Editorial. *La Civiltà Cattolica,* January 18, 2003.

Ortiz de Urbina, Ignacio. "Le origini del cristianesimo in Edessa." *Gregorianum* 15 (1934): 82–91.

Patulli Trythall, M. *Edmund Aloysius Walsh: La Missio Iraquensis. Il contributo dei Gesuiti Statunitensi al Sistema educativo iracheno. Studi sull'Oriente Cristiano* 14. Roma: Angelica-Costantiniana di Lettere Arti e Scienze, 2010.

Pius IX, Pope. *Aeterni Patris.* Bull. June 29, 1868.

———. *Arcana divina providentia.* Apostolic letter. September 8, 1868.

———. *Cum ecclesiastica disciplina*. Apostolic letter. August 31, 1869.

———. *Inter ea*. Apostolic letter. March 17, 1876.

Pontifical Council for the Promotion of Christian Unity. *Guidelines for Admission to the Eucharist Between the Chaldean Church and the Assyrian Church of the East*. July 20, 2001. http://www .vatican.va/roman_curia/pontifical_councils/chrstuni/ documents/rc_pc_chrstuni_doc_20011025_chiesa-caldea-assira_ en.html.

Rassam, Suha. *Christianity in Iraq*. Melbourne, Australia: Freedom Publishing, 2010.

Roberson, Ronald. *The Eastern Christian Churches*. Rome: Orientalia Christiana, 1999.

Sacrae Congregatio de Propaganda Fide. *Annales de l'Association de la Propagation de la Foi*. Vol. 2. 1826.

———. *Annales de la Propagation de la Foi*. Vols. 25 and 30. Lyon, 1853.

———. *Appendix Ad Bullarium Pontificium*. Vol. 1. Rome: Typis Collegii Urbani, n.d.

———. *Guide des Missions Catholiques*. Vol. 2. Paris: l'Œuvre Pontificale de la Propagation de la Foi, 1936.

Sacred Congregation for the Doctrine of the Faith, Congregation for the Eastern Churches, and Pontifical Council for Promoting Christian Unity. "Guide for the Admission to the Eucharist." *Information Service*, no. 108 (2001/IV): 149.

Sacred Congregation for the Eastern Churches. *Atti del Convegno di storia ecclesiastica contemporanea (Città del Vaticano, 22–24 ottobre 1998), La Questione armena: la Chiesa martire, in Fede e Martirio—Le Chiese orientali cattoliche nell'Europa del Novecento*. Vatican City: Libreria Editrice Vaticana, 2003.

———. *Oriente Cattolico—Cenni storici e statistiche*. Città del Vaticano: Sacra congregazione per le chiese orientali, 1974.

———. "La Questione armena: la Chiesa martire. Atti del Convegno di storia ecclesiastica contemporanea (Città del Vaticano, 22–24 ottobre 1998)." In *Fede e Martirio—Le Chiese orientali cattoliche nell'Europa del Novecento*. Vatican City: Libreria Editrice Vaticana, 2003.

Sako, L. *The Chaldean Catholic Church—A Story of Being*. Kirkuk, Iraq: privately published, 2009.

Sleiman, J. B. *Nella trappola irachena*. Milan: Paoline, 2007.

Soro, Mar Bawai. "The Rise of Eastern Churches and Their Heritage 5th–8th Century—Churches of Syriac Tradition II, The Assyrian (East Syriacs)." In *Christianity: A History in the Middle East,* ed. Habib Badr, 255–87. Beirut, Lebanon: Middle East Council of Churches, 2005.

Strazzari, F. *Dalla terra dei due fiumi Iraq-Iran—Cristiani tra l'integralismo e la Guerra.* Bologna: Edizioni Dehoniane Bologna, 2010.

Tucker, Mike. *Now We Are Free—Voices of the Kurds after Saddam.* Denver: Outskirts Press, 2014.

Valognes, J. P. *Vie et mort des chrétiens d'Orient—Des origines à nos jours.* L'Étang-La-Ville: Fayard, 1994.

Vaucelles, P. de. *La vie en Irak il y a un siècle vue par nos consuls.* Paris: 1965.

Vine, Aubrey R. *The Nestorian Churches: A Concise History of Nestorian Christianity in Asia from the Persian Schism to the Modern Assyrians.* London: Independent Press, 1937.

Wilmshurst, D. *The Ecclesiastical Organization of the Church of the East 1318–1913.* Leuven: Peeters, 2000.

Yacoub, Joseph. *I Cristiani d'Iraq.* Milan: Jaca Book, 2006.

———. *Qui s'en souviendra? 1915: le génocide assyro-chaldéo-syriaque.* Paris: Cerf, 2014.

Index

Baghdad, diocese of, 37, 42, 46, 48, 49, 52, 53, 55, 56, 57, 58, 62, 66, 65, 67, 69, 70, 71, 73, 77, 87, 88, 93, 103, 107, 114, 133, 138, 145, 148, 149, 152

Baghdad College, 136, 155

Baillet, Emmanuel, 61, 71, 74

Bardesanes, 11

Basidia, Shimon IV, 34, 35

Basra, 2, 12, 28, 30, 39, 43, 44, 46, 56, 59, 60, 62, 77, 78, 92, 101, 109, 114, 123, 142, 153, 165

Bernard de Saint Thérèse. See Duval, Jean

Berré, François Dominique, 116, 118, 121, 133, 134, 135, 136, 137, 138

Blair, Tony, 161

Britain, 4, 62, 77, 98, 99, 117, 123, 124, 125, 126, 127, 128, 130, 133, 139, 143, 144, 152, 159, 161, 170

Bush, George H. W., 175

Bush, George W., 161, 162

Byzantine Empire, 15, 19, 21, 24

Caliphate, 1, 22, 24, 26, 28, 30, 179, 180

Capuchins, 37, 44, 45, 47, 50, 51, 54, 57, 58, 59, 61, 63, 78, 82, 83, 84, 87, 89, 90, 102, 116, 117, 118, 135

Carmelites, 38, 43, 44, 45, 47, 48, 49, 50, 51, 52, 54, 55, 56, 58, 59, 60, 61, 62, 63, 65, 66, 68, 73, 78, 88, 92, 101, 107, 109, 114, 116, 128, 149, 168, 185

Castells, Nicolas, 73, 76, 81, 83, 84, 87, 88, 89, 92, 93, 101

Chaldeans, Church of, 1, 3, 10, 11, 21, 30, 34, 35, 37, 38, 40, 65, 66,

67, 68, 71, 72, 73, 82, 86, 97, 111, 113, 115, 121, 151, 156, 165, 167, 171, 174, 181; patriarch of, 37, 54, 63, 67, 69, 70, 71, 78, 79, 81, 82, 85, 90, 93, 96, 100, 103, 105, 112, 130, 133, 137, 141, 142, 146, 147, 149, 150, 155, 174, 176,

Church of the East, 6, 7, 9, 10, 11, 12, 16, 20, 21, 22, 23, 24, 26, 27, 29, 31, 32, 33, 34, 35, 36, 37, 40, 156, 164, 173, 174, 181; catholicos and patriarch of, 21, 23, 27, 29, 30, 32, 37

Constantinople, 49, 72, 75, 88, 93, 95, 96, 98, 99, 108, 113, 117, 136; church councils, 15, 16, 17, 18; patriarch of, 8, 17, 20, 26

Coupperie, Pierre-Alexandre, 66, 67, 68, 69, 71, 74, 92

Cyril of Alexandria, 17, 18, 132

Damascus, 3, 7, 26, 30, 33, 120, 180

Dominic (saint), 40

Dominicans, 1, 36, 38, 41, 45, 54, 58, 63, 64, 73, 85, 87, 90, 92, 93, 100, 101, 102, 104, 105, 106, 107, 108, 112, 114, 116, 118, 121, 127, 128, 130, 133, 134, 135, 138, 149, 152, 164, 167, 169, 170

Drapier, Antonin, 138, 139, 140, 141, 142, 145

Drure, François Désiré Jean, 114, 116, 117, 118, 127

Duval, Jean, 48, 50, 51, 52, 90

Eastern Churches, 16, 40, 42, 77, 80, 101, 103, 105; Congregations for the, 21, 42, 79, 80, 120, 122,

The Church in Iraq was designed and typeset in Minion Pro with Hypatia Sans by Kachergis Book Design of Pittsboro, North Carolina. It was printed on 60-pound House Natural Smooth, and bound by Sheridan Books of Chelsea, Michigan.